United States Government Accountability Office

Report to the Committee on Oversight and Government Reform, House of Representatives

May 2013

EMPLOYING PEOPLE WITH BLINDNESS OR SEVERE DISABILITIES

Enhanced Oversight of the AbilityOne Program Needed

GAO Highlights

Highlights of GAO-13-457, a report to the Committee on Oversight and Government Reform, House or Representatives

EMPLOYING PEOPLE WITH BLINDNESS OR SEVERE DISABILITIES:

Enhanced Oversight of the AbilityOne Program Needed

Why GAO Did This Study

In 1938, Congress created a program providing employment opportunities for people who are blind and expanded it in 1971 to include people with severe disabilities. Now known as AbilityOne, the program's public-private structure consists of the federal, independent U.S. AbilityOne Commission (15 part-time presidentially-appointed members supported by 27 staff) to oversee the program; two central nonprofit agencies (CNAs) to administer much of the program; and hundreds of affiliated nonprofit companies employing people who are blind or severely disabled to provide products and services to federal agencies. Federal agencies are generally required to purchase such products and services through the program.

GAO examined how the AbilityOne Commission: (1) directs and oversees the CNAs; (2) adds products and services (hereafter called projects) to the program and assigns affiliates to provide them; and (3) prices program projects. GAO reviewed policies, procedures, relevant federal laws and regulations, and other documents; interviewed CNA and AbilityOne officials; held five focus groups with affiliates; and analyzed data on program products, services, and pricing reviews.

What GAO Recommends

We are presenting a matter for Congressional consideration to establish an inspector general and several recommendations to the Commission to enhance program oversight. The Commission and CNAs agreed with our recommendations, but disagreed with several findings or provided additional information, which we incorporated as appropriate.

View GAO-13-457. For more information, contact Andrew Sherrill at (202) 512-7215 or sherrilla@gao.gov.

What GAO Found

Federal agencies need to exercise strong oversight to promote effectiveness and efficiency and prevent waste, fraud, and abuse—especially in a federal procurement program such as this, which is exempt from full and open competition requirements. However, although the AbilityOne Commission is ultimately responsible for overseeing the program, the Commission cannot control how CNAs (1) spend their funds, (2) set and manage their performance goals, or (3) set and implement governance policies and other internal controls. The Commission's authority to direct CNA budget priorities—including how much they compensate their executives and the level and growth of their reserves—is limited. As independent entities, the CNAs are responsible for determining their spending. Most of their money comes from fees they charge their affiliates as a percent of revenue earned from AbilityOne contracts. Moreover, the Commission does not have sufficient authority to set CNA performance and governance standards, so it depends on the CNAs to set and enforce such standards. Although the CNAs have instituted their own internal controls, the Commission does not have procedures to monitor alleged CNA control violations, nor is there an inspector general to provide independent audit and investigative capabilities for the program, including at the CNAs.

The AbilityOne Commission is responsible for determining which products and services can be suitably provided by the program. It delegates to the CNAs most of the responsibility for deciding which affiliates should develop and provide these projects. According to CNA and affiliate officials, the CNAs often do not fully disclose how they make these decisions. This limited transparency could increase the risk of biased decisions because CNA officials have wide latitude in determining which affiliate should be awarded a project. Although AbilityOne Commission officials have acknowledged the importance of transparency and equity in assigning projects, they have done little to indicate how these outcomes can be achieved.

The Commission has statutory responsibility for determining the fair market price of projects in the program, but: (1) its written pricing review policies and procedures are limited and (2) it does not have sufficient internal controls to ensure that prices are appropriately revised over time. The Commission sets procedures that encourage affiliates and federal customers to negotiate prices that reflect the market. Although Commission staff review these prices in accordance with written policies and procedures, they acknowledged that these instructions are not sufficiently explicit or transparent. Such limitations can make it difficult for the CNAs and affiliates to understand the Commission's pricing review procedures and, by extension, its reasons for rejecting prices. This lack of understanding may partially explain the 77 percent rejection rate for initial pricing packages. Commission policy also states that CNAs submit for Commission review any request for adjusting the price of a project beyond a single contract period that does not conform with the prior Commission-approved mechanism. Occasionally customers and affiliates implement non-conforming price revisions without requesting Commission approval. This negates the Commission's internal controls for ensuring fair market prices and results in the Commission not knowing the actual price being charged. Neither the AbilityOne Commission nor the CNAs have procedures in place to systematically identify such instances.

Contents

Abbreviations

CNA	Central Nonprofit Agency
FAR	Federal Acquisition Regulations
GDP	Gross Domestic Product
HHS	U.S. Department of Health and Human Services
IG	Inspector General
IRS	Internal Revenue Service
NIB	National Industries for the Blind
NISH	Formerly National Association for the Severely Handicapped
OMB	Office of Management and Budget
QWE	Quality Work Environment
SES	Senior Executive Service

U.S. GOVERNMENT ACCOUNTABILITY OFFICE

May 30, 2013

The Honorable Darrell Issa
Chairman
The Honorable Elijah E. Cummings
Ranking Member
Committee on Oversight and Government Reform
House of Representatives

Census data show that working-aged adults with severe disabilities have been employed at about one-third the rate as adults without disabilities.[1] Helping to mitigate this disparity, the AbilityOne Program creates employment opportunities for people who are blind or have severe disabilities through a unique public-private structure that connects such individuals to jobs that provide products and services to the federal government. Congress created this program in 1938 and it is now the single largest source of employment for people who are blind or have severe disabilities. In fiscal year 2012, this program provided jobs for approximately 48,000 such individuals and accounted for about $2.8 billion of federal procurements.

The AbilityOne Program relies on nonprofit agencies to employ people who are blind or have severe disabilities. These nearly 600 independent nonprofit affiliates are assisted by one of two private Central Nonprofit Agencies (CNAs): the National Industries for the Blind (NIB), which supports the creation of employment opportunities for people who are blind, and NISH, which supports the creation of employment opportunities for people with severe disabilities other than blindness.[2] The U.S. AbilityOne Commission oversees the CNAs and is ultimately responsible for the performance of the program.[3] The CNAs, in turn, manage much of

---

[1] For U.S. Census Bureau report on Americans with varied levels of disability, from none to severe, see Americans With Disabilities: 2010, http://www.census.gov/prod/2012pubs/p70-131.pdf.

[2] NISH was previously known as the National Industries for the Severely Handicapped, but now is officially known as NISH.

[3] The Committee for Purchase From People Who Are Blind or Severely Disabled is the independent federal agency that administers the AbilityOne program. This agency began using the name the U.S. AbilityOne Commission on October 1, 2011.

the day-to-day operations of the program, including working with affiliates to identify and recommend products and services that the Commission may want to add to the program and providing training and other support to their affiliates.

Federal agencies are required to obtain the products and services they need through the use of full and open competitive procedures, unless otherwise authorized by law.[4] Full and open competition promotes transparency and integrity within the federal procurement system because it allows for all responsible businesses that meet a customer's stated requirements to submit proposals in response to that customer's request for the product or service. In contrast, products and services procured through the AbilityOne Program are exempt from full and open competition requirements, but ensuring that the program is managed transparently and with integrity remains critically important. Such accountability must be ensured through appropriate levels of oversight and reporting of program operations. This includes overseeing the overall management and operations of the CNAs as well as ensuring that key program functions—such as determining which affiliate is assigned to provide a project and the pricing of those projects—are transparent. [5] Without this accountability, it is impossible to know the extent to which this uniquely structured public-private program is truly benefiting the blind and other persons with severe disabilities and whether federal customers are charged fair prices for the products and services they receive.

In light of the program's importance in creating employment opportunities for the disabled and its unique public-private structure, you asked us to examine some key aspects of the program's oversight. We focused on the following questions:

1. How does the AbilityOne Commission direct and oversee the CNAs and what limitations may exist with this oversight?

2. How are products and services added to the AbilityOne Program and how are providers of such projects assigned?

---

[4] Competition in Contracting Act of 1984, Pub. L. No. 98-369, § 2701.

[5] From this point on, we refer to both products and services produced through the AbilityOne Program as projects.

3. What processes does the AbilityOne Program follow when pricing projects?

To answer these questions, we reviewed the policies and procedures of the AbilityOne Commission and the CNAs, as well as their relevant reports, including annual business plans, annual financial statements and budget justifications, strategic plans, compensation studies, IRS Form 990s, as well as relevant federal laws and regulations.[6] We also interviewed officials from the AbilityOne Commission (members of the presidentially appointed Commission and senior staff) as well as officials from both CNAs (members of their boards of directors, senior executives, and senior staff). These interviews focused on: (1) how projects are added to the program, assigned to affiliates, and priced; (2) how the Commission oversees the CNAs; (3) concerns about project assignment, pricing, and oversight; and (4) how these concerns could be addressed. In addition, we spoke with 10 directors or managers of NISH affiliates about their perspectives on the AbilityOne Program and used this input in part to develop and conduct five focus groups. We conducted the focus groups with both NISH and NIB affiliates. To ensure that we obtained a range of viewpoints from the focus groups, four groups that we convened included affiliates that varied by size as well as their affiliated-CNA. The fifth focus group included affiliate directors who had appealed project assignment decisions. We spoke with 35 affiliates in all, in groups of 5 to 10. These group discussions focused on obtaining perspectives regarding the program in general and processes and practices associated with assigning and pricing projects in particular. To review the distribution of projects, we analyzed AbilityOne data on what projects were produced within the program and which affiliates produced them as of the end of fiscal year 2012. We assessed the reliability of these data and determined that they were sufficiently reliable for our purposes. Finally, we analyzed information from the Commission on the number and types of pricing reviews conducted between January 1, 2012 and December 10, 2012 (the latest period for which the Commission has data) and the outcome of these reviews.

---

[6] The Internal Revenue Service (IRS) requires nonprofit entities to annually submit a Form 990 that provides some basic information about the nonprofit, including its mission and governance structure; its balance sheet, income and expenses; and tax and financial information, such as whether its financial statements were audited by an independent accountant and compensation information on certain officers, directors, trustees, key employees, and the highest-compensated employees.

We conducted our work between February 2012 and May 2013, in accordance with generally accepted government auditing standards. Those standards require that we plan and perform the audit to obtain sufficient, appropriate evidence to provide a reasonable basis for our findings and conclusions based on our audit objectives. We believe that the evidence obtained provides a reasonable basis for our findings and conclusions based on our audit objectives.

Background

In 1938, Congress established a program under the Wagner-O'Day Act that created employment opportunities for the blind.[7] People employed under the program manufactured and sold certain products, such as brooms and mops, to the federal government. In 1971, Congress expanded the program under the Javits-Wagner-O'Day Act to employ people with other severe disabilities and provide services (in addition to products) to federal customers.[8] Today, the AbilityOne program provides more services than products. As of September 30, 2012, the program's list of projects (known as the Procurement List) included 4,639 projects— 65 percent of which were services and 35 percent of which were products. Services include janitorial, landscaping, and document destruction services as well as staffing call centers and base commissaries. Products include office and cleaning supplies, military apparel, and bedspreads. Federal agencies that need the specific products and services on the Procurement List are generally required to purchase them through the program.[9] Unlike contracts that are reserved exclusively for small businesses—which generally must be competed among qualified small businesses—contracts for projects on the Procurement List are not competed within the program. Once projects are included on this list, they can remain there indefinitely and continue to be provided by the initially-assigned affiliate.[10]

---

[7]Pub. L. No. 75-739, 52 Stat. 1196.

[8]Pub. L. No. 92-28, 85 Stat. 77.

[9]41 U.S.C. § 8504. The program allows for exceptions to such mandatory purchases, including when affiliated agencies cannot provide projects within timeframes federal customers require or when affiliates cannot economically provide the required quantity. See, e.g., 41 C.F.R. § 51-5.4.

[10]Federal contracting agencies may set aside, or reserve, an acquisition exclusively for participation by small business concerns. Small business concerns generally compete for these contracts.

The Organizational and Funding Structure of the AbilityOne Program

Three types of entities comprise the AbilityOne Program: (1) the AbilityOne Commission, (2) the CNAs, and (3) the affiliates. Figure 1 shows the program's organizational structure and how each of these entities is funded.

Figure 1: Organizational and Funding Structure of the AbilityOne Program

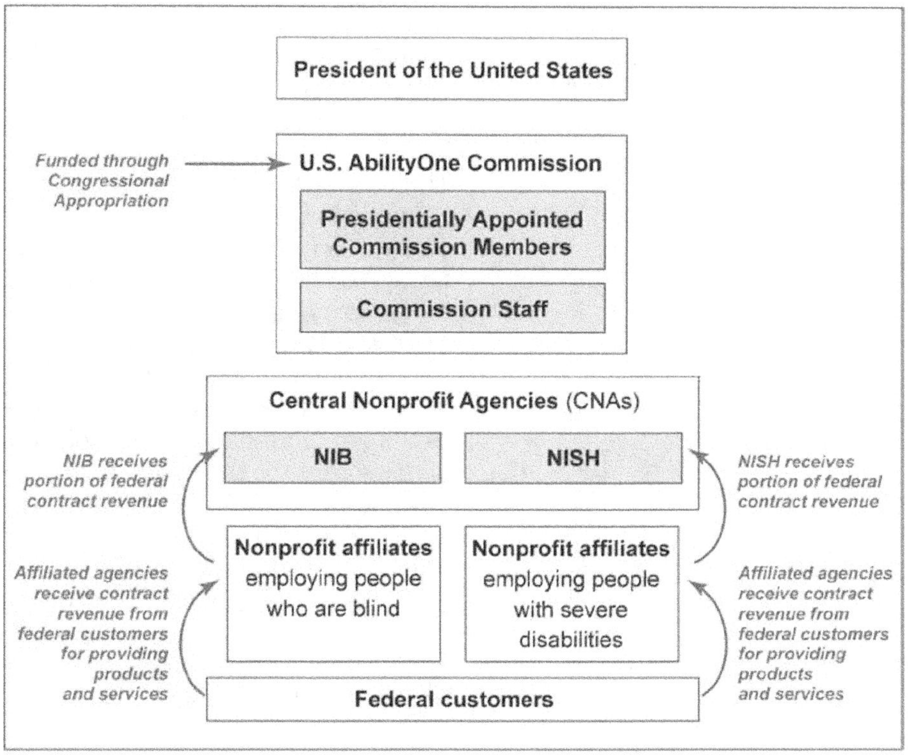

Source: GAO analysis of AbilityOne data.

The AbilityOne Commission consisted of a 15-member presidentially appointed Commission and 27 full-time staff as of the end of fiscal year 2012.[11] Its responsibilities include (1) establishing rules, regulations, and policies to assure the effective implementation of the program; (2) adding

---

[11] Eleven Commission members are representatives from federal agencies and four members are private citizens representing the interests of people who are blind or have severe disabilities.

new projects to the Procurement List, after determining whether they can be suitably provided by people who are blind or have severe disabilities; and (3) setting prices for these projects that reflect the market (fair market prices) and appropriately revising them over time. In regard to the CNAs, the Commission has the authority to (1) authorize and de-authorize one or more CNAs to help administer the program, (2) set the maximum fee ceiling the CNAs can charge their affiliates, and (3) provide guidance and technical assistance to the CNAs to ensure the successful implementation of the program. The Commission is funded through congressional appropriations which, in fiscal years 2011 and 2012 were almost $5.4 million each year.

The AbilityOne Commission designated two CNAs—NIB and NISH—to help administer the program. The Commission designated NIB in 1938 and in calendar year 2011, NIB had 161 employees and, as of the end of fiscal year 2012, NIB worked with 70 agencies affiliated with the program that employ people who are blind. The Commission designated NISH in 1974 and at the end of calendar year 2011, NISH had 352 employees and, as of the end of fiscal year 2012, NISH worked with 528 agencies affiliated with the program that employ people with severe disabilities. The CNAs are funded almost entirely through fees they charge their affiliates as a percentage of the revenues the affiliates earn from federal customers on AbilityOne contracts.

The affiliated agencies that provide AbilityOne projects to federal customers can be private nonprofit agencies or state-run nonprofit agencies. Some affiliates are part of well known nonprofit agencies, such as Goodwill Industries or Easter Seal agencies, and others are lesser known affiliates. Moreover, some affiliates rely exclusively or mostly on AbilityOne sales, whereas others have a substantial amount of sales outside of the AbilityOne Program. Regardless of how much business an affiliate conducts through the AbilityOne Program, the program requires that at least 75 percent of the total direct labor hours it uses to provide all products and services, including those outside of the AbilityOne Program, be carried out by people who are blind (in the case of NIB) or have severe disabilities or blindness (in the case of NISH).

The Commission Has Limited Control Over Some Aspects of CNA Operations

The Commission has limited authority to oversee and control the CNAs, which manage much of the program's day-to-day operations because they are independent nonprofit agencies. Even though the Commission has ultimate responsibility for program management and oversight because of the unique public-private structure of the program it cannot control how CNAs (1) spend their funds, (2) set and manage their performance goals, or (3) set and implement governance policies and other internal controls.

The Commission Has Limited Control Over CNA Spending

The Commission has limited influence over how CNAs spend their funds because the CNAs, as independent nonprofit entities, have their own boards of directors that determine how much the CNAs will spend on each item in their budgets. However, the Commission can influence the CNAs overall budgets by (1) reviewing CNA annual business plans and (2) limiting the maximum amount of revenue the CNAs can collect from their affiliates to fund their operations. Commission reviews of CNA business plans consist of examining the plans to ensure that they are aligned with the Commission's core goals and asking clarifying questions or requesting changes. The Commission limits CNA revenues by setting the maximum fee amount the CNAs can charge their affiliates based on revenues from their AbilityOne contracts.[12]

In fiscal year 2012, NISH spent $78 million and NIB spent $32 million on operations. The major expenses of each are depicted in figure 2 and all expenses are provided in appendix I.

---

[12] For regulations regarding the Commission's ability to set the CNA fee limit (also referred to as the fee ceiling) and the CNAs' ability to collect the fees, see 41 C.F.R. §§ 51-2.2(f), 51-3.5.

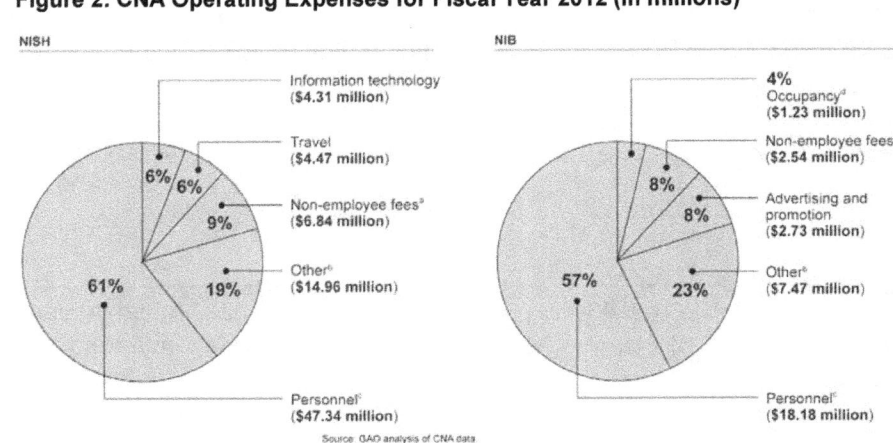

Figure 2: CNA Operating Expenses for Fiscal Year 2012 (in millions)

Source: GAO analysis of CNA data

[a] Fees for non-employee services include legal, accounting, investment management and other services.

[b] The other category includes a wide range of expenses, such as office expenses, insurance and other costs, which are identified in appendix I.

[c] The personnel category includes costs for the compensation of current officers and key employees, other salaries and wages, pension plan accruals and contributions, other employee benefits and payroll taxes.

[d] Occupancy expenses are for rent and utilities.

Because the CNAs are independent nonprofit agencies, the Commission's influence over their budgets does not and cannot extend to (1) controlling CNA cost areas, such as employee salaries and benefits or lobbying costs; (2) establishing a policy on the appropriate level of CNA reserves; and (3) ensuring that the CNAs provide sufficient funding to support key program initiatives designed to promote employment opportunities for people with severe disabilities.

Controlling Key CNA Cost Areas

Compensation and benefits. According to the Commission, it has no direct control over the amount that CNAs pay their executives and other employees, an important driver of CNA expenditures. In November 2004, the Commission proposed to exert more control through proposed regulations that included, among other things, standards regarding the reasonableness of executive and other employee compensation at the

CNAs.[13] The Commission eventually withdrew the entire regulatory proposal citing the number and nature of issues raised by commenters.[14]

Federal laws limit the amount of federal funds that can be used to pay the salaries of certain federal agency contractors and nonprofit agency executives receiving federal grants to the level II federal senior executive service (SES) salary, which in fiscal year 2012 was the maximum SES pay of $179,700.[15] CNA executive salaries, however, are not limited in this way because although the fees the affiliates pay the CNAs originate with federal customers, once they are remitted to the affiliates they are no longer federal funds. SES pay ranged from $119,554 to $179,700 in fiscal year 2012. Our review of the financial information submitted by NISH and NIB of their 25 highest-paid executives for this year shows that 11 executives had a salary above this range, 12 were within this range, and 2 were below this range. NISH and NIB employees, including the highest-paid executives, also received bonuses and benefits, such as pensions, and health, dental, disability, and life insurance. The highest-paid NISH executives as well as staff were entitled to first-class or business air travel in certain circumstances and reimbursement for eligible wellness program expenses up to a maximum of $250 annually.[16] Also, the NISH Chief Executive Officer received a stipend for a car.

---

[13] 69 Fed. Reg. 65,395 (Nov. 12, 2004). The Commission proposed to assess the reasonableness of compensation by considering a number of factors, such as the size and complexity of the CNA's mission, the compensation packages at other comparable affiliates or the other CNA, and the technical and professional qualifications required for the positions. In addition, the Commission also planned to consider the extent to which the executive compensation packages exceeded the total compensation offered to the typical, highest paid senior executive service (SES) career federal employee. If compensation exceeded this amount, the Commission planned to consider it unreasonable unless the CNA could provide justification for the compensation. The proposed regulatory changes were also intended to address the standards for assessing the reasonableness of compensation at the CNA affiliates.

[14] 70 Fed. Reg. 38,080 (July 1, 2005). The notice withdrawing the rule noted the Commission's intent to propose new regulations on this topic by the end of 2005, but the Commission has not taken any additional action in this area.

[15] Examples include people employed at Head Start agencies, people working in the Job Corps program, and people whose salaries originate with the Employment and Training Administration.

[16] First-class or business air travel is allowed by NISH only for uninterrupted flights of 8 hours or more or as a reasonable accommodation for an employee with a disability.

Within the last 5 years, each CNA has had different consultants conduct compensation assessments to determine whether their compensation was comparable to other organizations. The organizations used for comparison had similar missions and levels of revenue for the assessments conducted for NISH, and similar locations for the assessments conducted for NIB. These assessments took into consideration some factors similar to those in the Commission's proposed regulations, such as comparing the salary of job positions at the CNAs with positions at other organizations deemed similar. However, none of the assessments compared CNA compensation to federal sector compensation. One consultant who conducted one of the studies explained that this was because CNA job titles and functions were more comparable to the for-profit and nonprofit sectors than the federal sector. These assessments also varied in scope and methodology. For example, while some NISH assessments included a review of the value of all salary, cash incentives and benefits, the NIB assessments did not include a review of benefits. The 2011 study for NISH found that with the exception of salaries for three executives, the salaries of all NISH executives were comparable to the market median.[17] The 2009 study for NIB found, in part, that the salaries for NIB's leadership team needed to be increased to be competitive with the market, and NIB subsequently raised their salaries.[18]

Lobbying. Another CNA budgetary area which the Commission cannot control is the extent of lobbying conducted by NIB and NISH. Federal agencies generally cannot use federal appropriations to lobby Congress,[19] and the Federal Acquisition Regulation (FAR) limits reimbursement of federal government contractors' lobbying and political activity costs.[20] NISH and NIB are under no such restriction, however. The income NISH and NIB receive through fees from federal contracts are not appropriated funds, thus they may use these fees or other income to fund their lobbying efforts. For 2012, NIB reported spending $175,729

---

[17] The salary for three executives ranged from being: (1) above the competitive range of the 75th percentile, (2) within the competitive range for the 75th percentile, and (3) between the competitive range of the 50th and 75th percentile.

[18] The NIB study found that the salaries for NIB's leadership team were at 79 percent of the market median.

[19] 18 U.S.C. § 1913.

[20] FAR § 31.205-22.

GAO-13-457 Review of the AbilityOne Program

and NISH reported spending $700,000 on lobbying.[21] In the same period, NIB reported lobby activities related to the AbilityOne Program, the Rehabilitation Act, Social Security and federal procurement, and NISH reported lobbying related to 10 different bills or laws.[22] Over the last 5 years, from 2008 to 2012, NIB reporting spending about $976,729 and NISH reported spending $3.5 million on lobbying.

Establishing a Policy on Appropriate Reserve Levels

Because the CNAs are independent nonprofit agencies, the Commission also lacks direct control over the amounts CNAs set aside as reserves. Reserves are important to ensure that an organization has sufficient funds to meet changing cash flow requirements. However, in the case of the AbilityOne Program, it is also important that the CNAs do not retain excess reserves that could be used to maintain and develop the program. A member of the Commission told us, for example, that the CNAs have generally been accumulating reserve funds, even though his expectation was that the dollar amount of reserves should fluctuate in both positive and negative directions as opposed to simply continue to grow. Although the Commission has the authority to adjust the CNAs' fee limits which could be used to curb unnecessary growth in the CNAs' entire budgets over time, this authority does not result in direct control over CNA reserve levels. Moreover, beyond the Commission's written guidance that CNA annual business plans report their level of reserves and how they will use any surplus revenue to accomplish strategic goals, the Commission has not provided written guidance to the CNAs about what they should consider when setting their reserve policies. The Commission also has not requested that the CNAs provide financial analyses that fully support their level of current reserves and their reserve policies.[23] Since NISH and NIB have different reserve policies, a comparison of reserves held by

---

[21] Federal law requires lobbyists to file quarterly lobbying disclosure reports and semiannual reports on certain political contributions. 2 U.S.C. § 1604.

[22] Some of the bills for which NISH reported lobbying activities before congressional bodies included: (1) the Acquisition Savings Reform Act of 2011, S. 1736, 112th Cong. (2011); (2) the Fair Wages for Workers with Disabilities Act of 2011, H.R. 3086, 112th Cong. (2011); and (3) the Workforce Investment Improvement Act of 2012, H.R. 4297, 112th Cong. (2012).

[23] According to the Commission, to decrease reserves the Commission reduced CNA fee limits in fiscal year 2007.

each CNA is inappropriate.[24] Figure 3, however, shows the trend in reserves for NISH and NIB separately over time. Specifically, the annual reserves for NISH for fiscal years 2008 to 2012 as well as its reserve projection for fiscal year 2013 continued to grow, while NIB's reserves declined slightly in 2011and 2013 (see fig. 3).

Figure 3: NISH and NIB Reserves for Fiscal Years 2008 to 2013

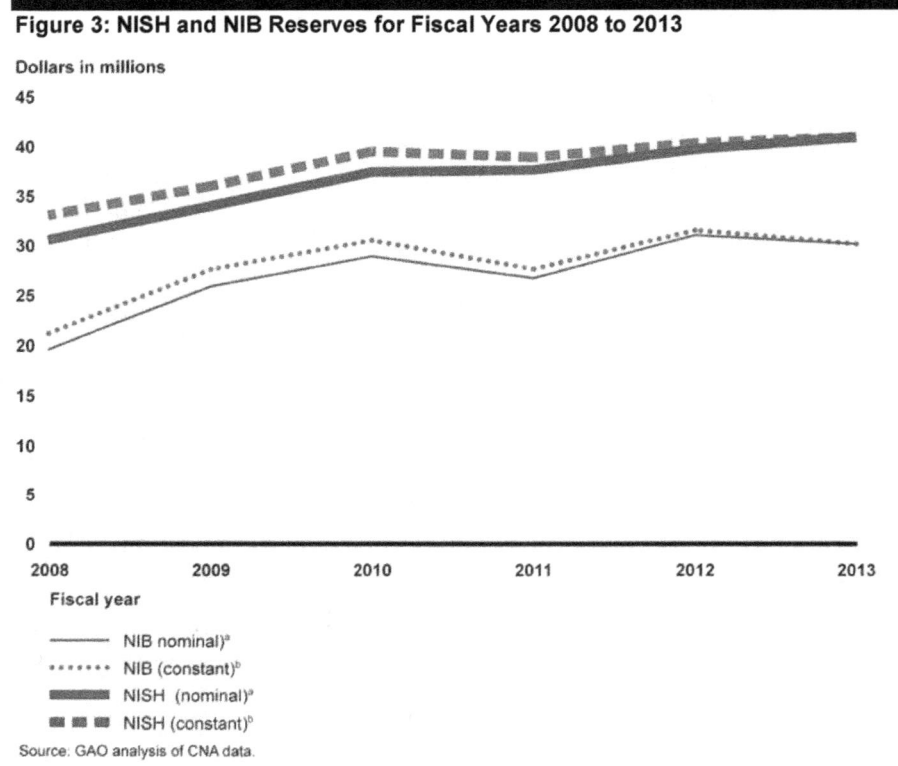

Dollars in millions

Fiscal year

— NIB nominal)ᵃ
...... NIB (constant)ᵇ
■■■ NISH (nominal)ᵃ
■■■ NISH (constant)ᵇ

Source: GAO analysis of CNA data.

[a]NISH (nominal) and NIB (nominal) data are the actual data from NISH or NIB from certified financial statements for fiscal years 2008 through 2012 and the budget data are for fiscal year 2013.

[b]NISH (constant dollars) and NIB (constant dollars) data have been inflated for fiscal years 2008 through 2012 using fiscal year 2013 as the base year and fiscal year Gross Domestic Product (GDP) index projections from the Congressional Budget Office, The Budget and Economic Outlook (Washington, D.C.: Feb. 2013).

[24] NISH's reserve policy is to target 6 months of its annual expense budget in cash and investments. NIB's policy is to reserve 6 to 12 months of its annual expense budget in net assets. In recent years, NISH has been somewhat below its 6-month target and NIB has exceeded its upper limit once in the last 8 years.

GAO-13-457 Review of the AbilityOne Program

Ensuring CNA Funding of Program Initiatives	While AbilityOne officials told us that the CNAs have generally supported the Commission's leadership of the program, including the funding of key initiatives, they also said that at any time the CNAs could become unsupportive and decide that they do not want to move in the Commission's direction. This situation exists in part because the CNAs, as private independent entities, determine how to spend their own funds. Thus, instead of requiring the CNAs to take certain actions to support the program, the Commission often has to seek their voluntary cooperation. In 2009, for example, according to CNA officials, the Commission tried to mandate CNA participation in its quality work environment (QWE) initiative to improve employee satisfaction and expected the CNAs to immediately incorporate funding for it into their budgets. However, CNA officials told us that the Commission did not have the authority to require such participation. According to Commission officials, this type of response from the CNA officials demonstrates the Commission's past and ongoing problems with trying to exert control over CNA spending. CNA officials explained that they needed time to develop implementation plans and determine the level of financial support they would provide before determining how to include it in their budgets. While the CNAs reported that they have continually funded QWE since its first year, AbilityOne officials still remain concerned about their lack of authority to require and enforce program improvements and the potential for future resistance from the CNAs.

CNA officials also pointed out that they have routinely provided non-inherently governmental support to the AbilityOne Program.[25] For fiscal year 2013, NIB budgeted $600,000 to provide support to the program in five areas: (1) information management, (2) technical writing, (3) communications and collaboration among program partners, (4) publications, and (5) distributors for AbilityOne services. For example, NIB plans to provide a communications manager to strengthen collaboration and communication among AbilityOne partners and to provide additional assistance to expand the number of distributors for various AbilityOne services, such as food and janitorial services. For fiscal years 2013 and 2014, NISH plans to provide assistance in six areas: (1) information systems coordination and integration, (2) AbilityOne

---

[25] AbilityOne regulations require the CNAs to perform various administrative functions, including activities to increase awareness of the program. 41 C.F.R. § 51-3.2. Non-inherently governmental functions are functions that a government agency can contract or pay an external party to perform.

web site support, (3) communications, (4) research, (5) program awards, and (6) brand management. NISH estimated that it spent $1.8 million for fiscal year 2012 and will spend $1.6 million for fiscal year 2013 for this type of support.

The Commission Has Limited Authority over CNA Performance Management, Governance Standards, and Other Internal Controls

Overseeing CNA Performance Management

The Commission has set and monitored a limited number of strategic overall program goals and performance standards (specific measures and targets), but because it has limited authority, it relies on the CNAs to set and monitor their own performance standards. During our last review of the program and its overall goals published in 2007, the program had five strategic goals and more than 30 performance measures that were not clearly defined or were difficult to measure, which made it difficult to assess performance.[26] However, the Commission has made substantial progress in addressing these weaknesses by further reducing its goals to focus on four core program areas: (1) effective stewardship; (2) customer and employee satisfaction; (3) employment growth; and (4) business excellence.[27] The CNAs have used these core program areas to develop their performance measures and targets. While the Commission is aware of the CNA performance measures and targets, it cannot revise them to help manage CNA performance. Thus, even when the Commission believed that one CNA performance target—15 percent annual growth in AbilityOne services—could not be achieved; the Commission could not require that the target be changed.

Overseeing Governance Standards

The Commission has not recently taken an active role in setting or monitoring CNA governance standards—such as developing CNA ethics

---

[26] GAO, *Federal Disability Assistance: Stronger Federal Oversight Could Help Assure Multiple Programs' Accountability*, GAO-07-236 (Washington, D.C.: Jan. 26, 2007).

[27] For the AbilityOne fiscal years 2010 to 2014 Strategic Plan, see http://www.abilityone.gov/media_room/publications.html.

standards and reviewing alleged violations—to help protect the program from possible waste, fraud, and abuse. Instead, the Commission is dependent upon the CNAs themselves, as well as other governmental entities, such as the Internal Revenue Service, to set and enforce some of these standards. In November 2004, the Commission published proposed rules that would have imposed some governance standards upon the CNAs, but later withdrew the proposal citing the number and nature of the objections raised by commenters. In the proposed regulatory changes, the Commission proposed to incorporate a number of governance standards that would limit membership on the CNAs' boards and address conflict of interest policies, among other things. For example, the Commission proposed to ensure that the Chairperson of the Board of a CNA was not also the Chief Executive Officer, President, or Executive Director of the CNA or any of its affiliates. Also, the Commission proposed that the CNAs and their affiliates adopt conflict of interest policies and disclose board members' business relationships with the CNA. According to AbilityOne Commission senior officials, the Commission has not made another attempt to formulate governance standards because they do not believe they have sufficient legal authority or resources to enforce them. Without strong standards and oversight, however, the program is vulnerable to potential fraud, waste, and abuse of government procurement funds. Moreover, should such improprieties occur, the program's reputation could be harmed and this could decrease employment opportunities for people who are blind or have severe disabilities.

According to NIB officials, other nonprofit boards, such as Goodwill Industries, United Way, and Easter Seals, have chosen to minimize their conflict of interest exposure by not having a majority of their directors employed by a related nonprofit. NIB and NISH, however, have decided to allow half or more of their board members to be executives or employees of affiliates in the program.[28] Both CNAs recognize that the makeup of their boards increases the risk of possible conflicts of interest on the part of their boards. The CNAs have, therefore, taken several steps to help mitigate these risks. For example, to reduce the potential for conflict of interest, the CNAs no longer have their boards involved in day-

---

[28] According to a NIB official, employees or executives of a NIB affiliate cannot serve as officers on NIB's board, but those individuals can serve on the board.

to-day management decisions, such as determining which affiliate would be assigned to develop a potential project.

Overseeing CNA Internal Controls

The Commission plays a limited role in overseeing how well CNAs are implementing their own internal controls. Even though the Commission has delegated the performance of much of the program's day-to-day activities to the CNAs, as the independent federal agency over the program, it is responsible for overseeing the CNAs to ensure that all applicable government standards are met. For example, under the standards for internal controls in the federal government, management must continually assess and evaluate its internal controls to assure that the control activities being used are effective and updated when necessary to effectively manage the program to achieve its goals and avoid potential for waste, fraud, or abuse.[29] Although the Commission does have high-level efforts in place to oversee the CNAs' ability to achieve the program's strategic goals, it has not—as suggested in the Office of Management and Budget (OMB) circular on management and accountability of federal programs[30]—made certain that it has, or that the CNAs have, controls in place at the CNAs that are appropriate and cost-effective. For example, the Commission relies heavily on CNA recommendations regarding which affiliate should provide an AbilityOne project. However, the Commission has not reviewed the controls the CNAs have in place to help ensure that the information the CNAs provide in support of these recommendations is accurate, complete, and not influenced by conflicts of interest.

The CNAs perform audits and reviews of their internal controls and collect information on allegations of misconduct or potential internal control violations reported through their whistleblower or other mechanisms, such as their review of CNA employee conflict of interest forms. Both CNAs have had independent financial and human resource audits conducted as well as recent audits of their procurement systems. NISH has also performed an internal risk assessment, but NIB has not conducted such an assessment in the last 5 years. The Commission has not reviewed findings from any of the CNA audits and assessments, with the exception of CNA financial audits. Such reviews would allow the Commission to

---

[29] See GAO, *Internal Control Management and Evaluation Tool,* GAO-01-1008G (Washington, D.C.: Aug. 2001), p. 5.

[30] See OMB circular A-123 at: http://www.whitehouse.gov/omb/circulars_a123_rev.

know where there are weaknesses in any CNA internal controls and ensure that CNA plans to address them are adequate and implemented in a timely manner. Similarly, the Commission does not generally review information about allegations of misconduct or potential internal control violations collected by the CNAs. Such reviews are important, given that the Commission runs this program through which about $2.9 billion in federal contracting flowed in fiscal year 2012. However, the CNAs do not routinely provide to the Commission information on alleged misconduct or internal control violations at either CNA or their affiliates, with a few exceptions. The primary exception is when the allegation is related to the functions for which the Commission is specifically responsible, such as the requirement that at least 75 percent of an affiliate's direct labor is performed by people who are blind or have severe disabilities. In this situation, the CNAs will report the allegation to the Commission. Commission officials have cited their limited authority and limited staff resources, in comparison to the much larger CNAs, as reasons why it is not able to fully review the CNAs' internal control activities.

Enhancing Federal Oversight and Control of the AbilityOne Program

As we previously discussed, the Commission lacks sufficient authority and procedures to help ensure the effectiveness, efficiency, and integrity of CNA operations. One option to address this situation would be for the Commission to enter into a written agreement with each CNA that specifies key expectations for the CNA and mechanisms for the Commission to oversee their implementation. No such agreement is currently in place. An agreement of this kind could enhance program oversight and accountability by providing more specificity about the responsibilities, processes, and relevant consequences to which the parties have agreed. However, it is possible that an agreement might not be reached since the Commission cannot compel the CNAs to enter into agreements and the CNAs may have little motivation to enter into an agreement that may limit their autonomy. Therefore, the Commission would need to deal with such a possibility. The Commission's primary source of leverage with regard to the CNAs is its ability to replace current CNAs with other agencies. In the event that the Commission could not reach agreement with a CNA on the provisions needed to provide an appropriate level of oversight and accountability for the AbilityOne program, then the Commission may need to take steps to designate a CNA that is willing to enter into such an agreement. The Commission could also seek legislation that would require such an agreement to be a prerequisite for being designated as a CNA.

Commission officials told us that they would need additional resources to establish and oversee written agreements with CNAs and that one alternative for funding could be to redirect receipt of a portion of the fees collected by the CNAs to the Commission. If this alternative were considered, additional controls over program funding would be needed to prevent a potential conflict of interest for the Commission—namely that the Commission could influence its funding level by increasing the maximum fee amount the CNAs could charge their affiliates. Such controls could include Congress mandating a maximum amount of funding the Commission could obtain from the fees or changes to how the Commission sets the fees.

Another option to improve federal oversight of the program—including reviewing CNA internal control activities and compliance with program rules and regulations—would be to create an independent inspector general (IG) with the authority to audit and investigate the Commission and the CNAs. An IG could follow up, as needed, on allegations of misconduct or internal control violations. It could also identify ways to improve the efficiency and effectiveness of the CNAs' internal controls. Additionally, it could identify broader issues that could arise within the program, such as affiliate noncompliance with program requirements and oversight of the AbilityOne Commission itself.[31] Although IG findings and recommendations could be used to help persuade CNAs to address a problem, AbilityOne officials believe that they would also need a mechanism that would give them the ability to implement any recommended IG changes, such as the written agreements described above.

---

[31] For an example of noncompliance by AbilityOne Program affiliates, see GAO-07-236.

The Commission Relies on CNAs to Recommend Projects for the Program, but Has Not Resolved Concerns about How CNAs Assign Projects to Affiliates

The Commission relies on CNA recommendations when determining which projects are added to the AbilityOne Procurement List and when assigning affiliates to provide them. However, some affiliates have expressed concerns that CNA assignment decisions may not be sufficiently transparent or equitable. In response to these concerns, the AbilityOne Commission issued a policy on how CNAs should assign projects. While a step in the right direction, this policy may be ineffective in several ways.

CNAs Assign Affiliates to Develop Potential Projects and Recommend Projects for Review to the Commission

Federal law gives the AbilityOne Commission the authority to add projects to the AbilityOne Program Procurement List and federal regulations give the Commission the authority to approve which agencies affiliated with the program can provide the projects. In so doing, the Commission relies heavily on recommendations from the CNAs. Specifically, it takes five steps to add a project to the Procurement List (see fig. 4).

Figure 4: Major Steps in Adding Projects to the AbilityOne Procurement List

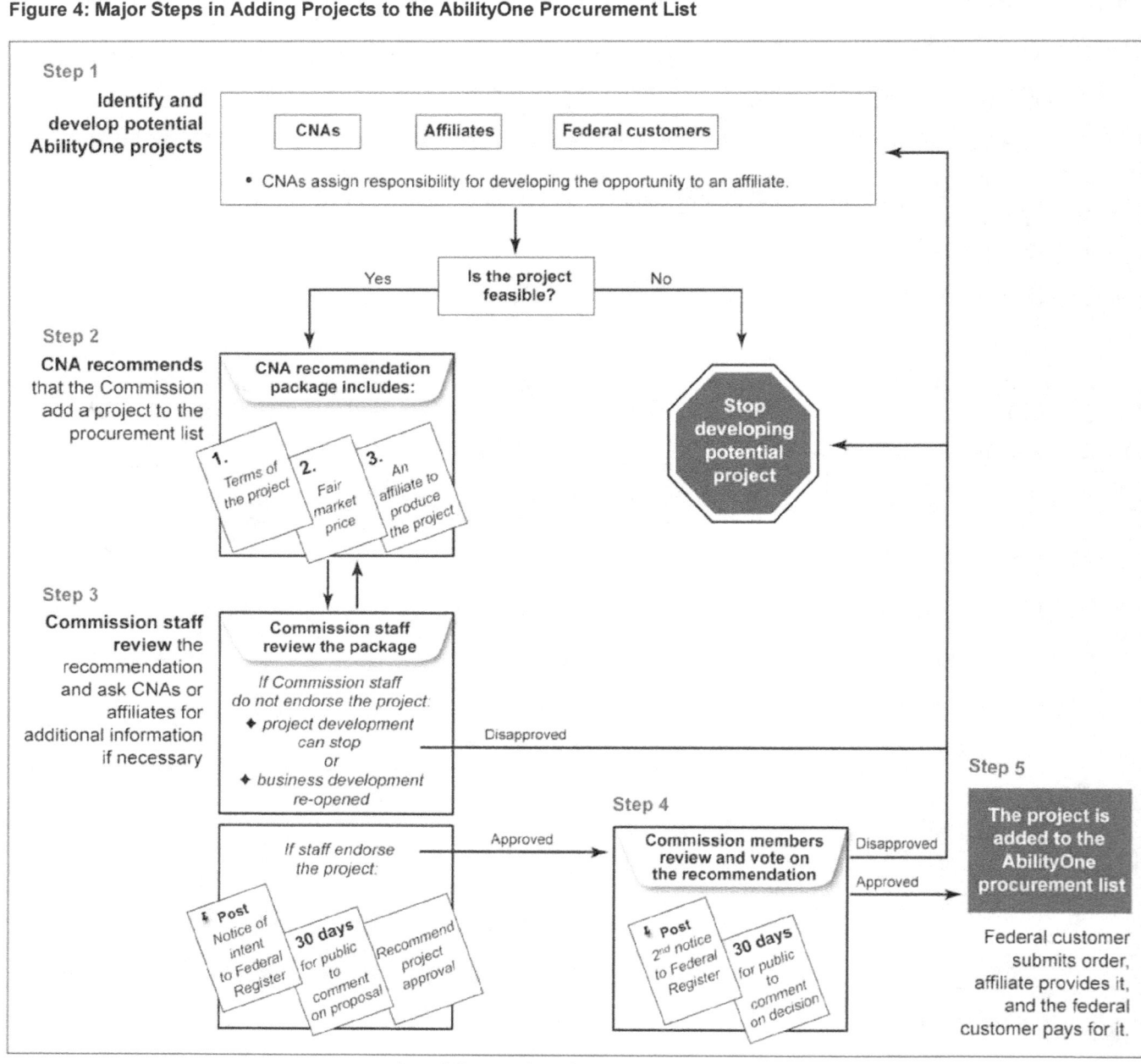

Source: GAO analysis of AbilityOne data.

GAO-13-457 Review of the AbilityOne Program

Under the first step of the Procurement List addition process, the CNAs assign one of their affiliated agencies to develop a business opportunity that potentially may become an AbilityOne project, in accordance with their own procedures. The Commission does not provide input into which affiliate is assigned at this stage. In step 2, the CNAs recommend that the Commission add the potential project to the Procurement List using a standard project addition package. The affiliate that the CNA assigns to develop the potential project is typically the affiliate that the CNA recommends to the Commission to provide the project in this package. In step 3, Commission staff review CNA addition packages to determine whether the project is suitable for the AbilityOne Program, using the criteria in the sidebar. According to Commission staff, they do not determine: a) whether another affiliate would be better positioned to provide the project or b) if the CNAs followed appropriate processes in selecting the affiliate. In step 4, Commission members vote on whether to add staff-recommended projects to the Procurement List, using the same four criteria that staff used to evaluate the project. They also vote on whether the CNA-recommended affiliate should be designated to provide the project. According to Commission staff, members vote to add the vast majority of projects staff put forward for addition to the Procurement List.

The Processes CNAs Use to Assign Projects Are Not Fully Transparent and Some Affiliates View Them as Inequitable

GAO has identified key elements that public procurement systems should have to ensure that they are efficient and accountable. Two of these, which the Commission has also acknowledged in policy as being important in the AbilityOne Program, are: [32]

• transparency, which includes having written procedures that are easily understandable by all; and
• equity, which includes maintaining impartiality, avoiding conflict of interest and preferential treatment, and dealing fairly and in good faith with all parties. [33]

---

[32] See U.S. AbilityOne Commission, Policy 51.301, "Selection of Nonprofit Agencies for Project Assignment and Order Allocation," (Arlington, VA: May 30, 2012). This policy applies to both the assignment of projects to affiliates at the business development stage and allocation of projects among affiliates that are added to the Procurement List.

[33] GAO, *District of Columbia: Procurement System Needs Major Reform*, GAO-07-159 (Washington, D.C.: Jan. 19, 2007). This report refers to this element as integrity. The explanation given for integrity in this report matches how we explained equity during the course of our work. Specifically, we defined equity as being free from bias or favoritism.

The processes the CNAs use to make assignment decisions allow them to exercise discretion when determining which affiliate to assign to a project and such discretion can limit transparency and equity. A Commission official told us that such discretion is essential to balancing the core mission of this program—providing employment opportunities for people who are blind or have severe disabilities—with providing quality projects to federal agencies in a timely and economical manner. AbilityOne officials also told us that their involvement in determining which affiliate should provide a project is limited. The reasons they gave for relying so heavily on CNA recommendations include (1) historically, project assignment has always been a CNA responsibility, and (2) it is the CNAs that have the necessary expertise to assess which affiliates are best suited to providing specific projects.

Although both NISH and NIB have written procedures for assigning affiliates to projects, some affiliates told us that they do not always find the CNAs' assignment processes transparent. Both CNAs have basic eligibility criteria that all affiliates must meet or they will be disqualified from pursuing a potential project. NISH has 16 additional criteria that it uses when making assignment decisions among qualifying affiliates and NIB has 7 (see sidebar). Both NISH and NIB also provide feedback to affiliates that were not awarded a project, upon request.

NISH officials explained that not all of its criteria are relevant when determining which affiliate should be assigned a project and that each project notification lists those criteria that will be used. NIB officials explained that due to the general nature of their criteria, most are applicable to assignment decisions. Nevertheless, some NISH and NIB affiliates told us that they do not always understand how the CNAs apply the assignment criteria on a project-by-project basis and, as a result, do not understand how their proposals are being judged. One affiliate explained, for example, that sometimes his CNA views geographic proximity to a project's worksite as more important than prior experience in a relevant line of business when evaluating affiliate proposals and sometimes they do the opposite. However, because the CNA does not tell the affiliates up front which criteria will be weighted as more important, affiliates do not know what elements to emphasize in their proposals and can be confused as to why one affiliate was assigned a project over another affiliate.

Moreover, some affiliates have questioned the overall integrity of the CNAs' assignment processes. Several affiliates we spoke with stated that they feel the system is biased in that assignment decisions tend to favor larger affiliates, affiliates that are or were on one of the CNAs' boards of directors, or are a member of a particular affiliate sub-group. In addition, NISH assignment decisions are made by a regional executive director in each of its six regions and some affiliates questioned whether these individuals apply NISH assignment criteria consistently.

Affiliates have also said that when NIB identifies a potential project for development, NIB does not routinely notify all affiliates. Instead, NIB usually notifies only those that they think may be interested in, and capable of, developing it. During our focus groups with affiliates, several mentioned that this practice can make it difficult for them to be considered for a different or new line of business. NISH, on the other hand, routinely notifies all affiliates of potential projects through its website and such notification is a requirement in NISH assignment procedures.

Limited Transparency and Perceived Inequities in Project Distribution May Not Be Resolved by the Commission's Most Recent Efforts

The Commission's May 2012 policy, according to Commission officials, sought to articulate a minimum set of broad principles that CNA assignment policies and procedures should incorporate—some of which relate to the elements of transparency and equity discussed above. This was the first time that the Commission had issued a written policy to guide CNA project assignment decisions, although the CNAs have had their own written procedures for years. Commission officials told us that they issued this written policy for two reasons. First, in the event that an affiliate filed suit in court over an assignment decision, as occurred in 2010, the Commission wanted to be able to point to a written policy that described how they expect CNAs to make assignment decisions.[34] Second, they felt that having a written policy was important, given complaints levied by some affiliates that CNA assignment decisions sometimes lacked transparency and appeared biased. A Commission official acknowledged that the principles articulated in its assignment policy generally aligned with the CNAs' written procedures. As a result, the Commission did not expect that the CNAs would need to make substantial changes in their assignment processes.

---

[34] An affiliate filed an appeal with the United States Court of Federal Claims challenging a contract award to another affiliate on several grounds. See Bona Fide Conglomerate v. United States, 96 Fed. Cl. 233 (2010). The court ultimately dismissed the claim because the AbilityOne Commission took corrective action by setting aside the award and pursuing a new source selection process.

Our review of the Commission's policy shows that although it describes some desired outcomes regarding CNA assignment decisions, it does little to indicate how these outcomes can be achieved. For example:

- The policy states that CNAs should develop processes to assure that projects are distributed among affiliates that result in fair, equitable, and transparent distribution, taking into account the unique mission and objectives of the program. It does not explore how such distribution should be achieved, or define what is meant by fair, equitable, and transparent.
- To maintain CNA discretion in determining certain criteria to use when making decisions, the policy allows decisions to be at least partially based on special considerations in certain circumstances. The policy gives examples of special considerations, such as providing jobs to wounded warriors or using environmentally friendly supplies, but it does not limit the CNAs to them. The policy also does not define or provide any examples of the circumstances in which the special considerations may be applied, which limits transparency. The policy also lacks transparency because it does not require that the CNAs routinely disclose to affiliates applying for projects how and why special considerations were used in making assignment decisions. Instead, it says that upon the Commission's request, CNAs must certify that an assignment complies with all applicable policies and procedures and include documentation about any special circumstances in the project addition package submitted to the Commission.

The policy also contains three types of enforcement mechanisms, another key internal control intended to ensure that program directives are followed, but they are not well—formulated. [35] Specifically:

- The policy requires that the Commission review CNA assignment processes at least once every 3 years to determine whether these processes are aligned with the principles outlined in its policy. However, because some of the principles contained in this policy are vague, the Commission may have difficulty determining the extent to which CNA procedures are aligned with them. Although the policy

---

[35] One internal control standard is control activities. Internal control activities are the policies, procedures, techniques, and mechanisms that help ensure that management's directives to mitigate risks identified during the risk assessment process are carried out. See GAO-01-1008G, p. 33.

states that these reviews would begin in 2012, as of February 2013 the Commission had not developed review procedures or conducted any reviews.

- The policy requires that CNAs document any special considerations that figure into an assignment decision and provide such documentation to the Commission upon request. It does not, however, specify what the documentation should entail. For example, it does not require the CNA to document why or how a particular consideration was used in an assignment decision. Such information would be critical to assessing whether the assignment decision was impartial and free from bias.
- The policy requires that CNAs have written appeal processes in place and both CNAs had such written procedures before to the Commission issued its policy. The policy also requires that the AbilityOne Commission develop its own separate written appeals policy and procedures, which would allow for a second level of appeal. At the time of our review the Commission did not have a timeline for developing this policy.

The Commission Does Not Track How the Program's Distribution of Projects Affects Job Creation for Its Target Population

The AbilityOne Commission has not determined how the assignment of projects among affiliates has affected the creation of employment opportunities for people who are blind or have severe disabilities and, according to Commission officials, has not done so at least in part because of limited resources. Such an assessment is important to conduct for two reasons. First, identifying risks that may affect the capacity of an agency to meet its mission—in this case the creation of jobs for people who are blind or have severe disabilities—is an important internal control.[36] Because the Commission has not determined if or how the current assignment of projects affects its mission, it does not know whether the way projects are currently distributed among affiliates poses a risk to achieving the program's mission and, if so, the extent of this risk. Second, according to an AbilityOne official, the relationship between the distribution of projects and job creation for people who are blind or have severe disabilities has been an ongoing debate among affiliates, CNAs, and the Commission for years.

AbilityOne and CNA officials told us that there is no clear research to indicate whether the current distribution of projects among affiliates

---

[36] See GAO-01-1008G, p. 23.

affects the amount of employment opportunities created for people who are blind or have severe disabilities. On the one hand, AbilityOne and CNA officials said that the program could benefit from spreading projects widely among its affiliates. Under this scenario, the program would not be as reliant on the capabilities of a few affiliates to hire people who are blind or have severe disabilities. Such a broad bench of affiliates may reduce the possibility of the program losing a federal customer if a producing affiliate becomes unable to provide a project because the project could be transferred to another affiliate within the program that had similar or potentially similar capabilities and capacity. On the other hand, Commission and CNA officials also said there could be benefits from a completely different distribution that assigned relatively more projects to some of the largest affiliates. Larger affiliates typically have more experience and their size creates economies of scale necessary to provide large projects, such as computer destruction or contract closeout services for an entire federal agency or program within an agency.

We analyzed fiscal year 2012 program data and found that while the largest affiliates represent a minority of the AbilityOne affiliates, they hold the majority of projects. Figure 5 shows that the largest 114 affiliates (20 percent) that provided projects as of the end of fiscal year 2012 had 56 percent of the projects and 79 percent of the sales dollars.[37]

---

[37] Distribution results vary if different–sized sale categories are used; however, the trend continues to be that the largest affiliates hold the majority of projects.

Figure 5: Distribution of Projects among Different-Sized Affiliates

Number of affiliates per size category[a]	Percent of different-sized affiliates	Percent of AbilityOne projects	Percent of AbilityOne sales
Large (114)	20	56	79
Mid-size (114)	20	20	14
Small (342)	60	24	7

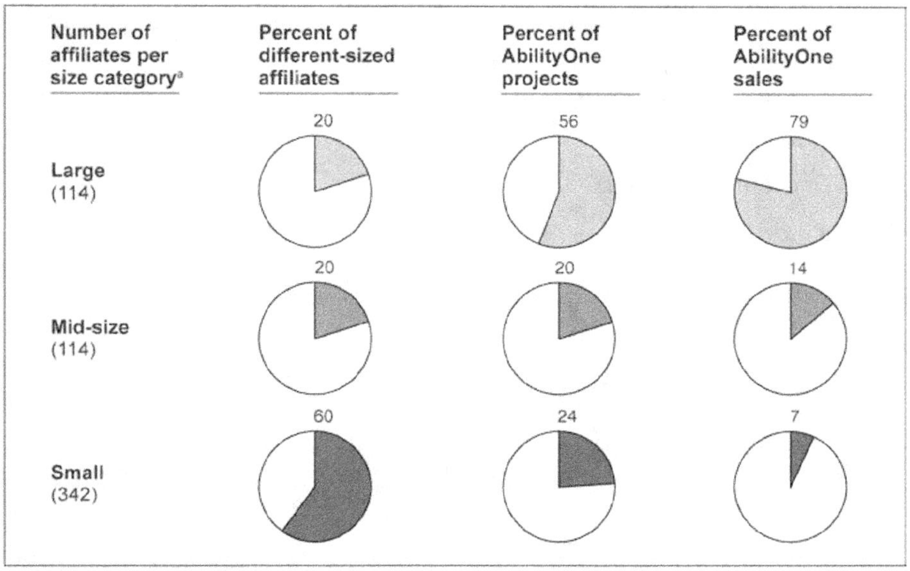

Source: GAO analysis of AbilityOne data.

[a] Size categories are based on total affiliate sales, which are AbilityOne plus non-AbilityOne sales. Median total sales for small affiliates was $996 thousand and ranged from $8 thousand to $3.38 million; median total sales for mid-size affiliates was $5.8 million and ranged from $3.4 million to $9.87 million; and median total sales for large affiliates was $18.2 million and ranged from $9.9 to $248.2 million.

We also analyzed the distribution of projects among NIB and NISH affiliates separately. The largest 13 NIB affiliates (20 percent) held 46 percent of AbilityOne projects and 53 percent of AbilityOne sales. The largest 100 NISH affiliates (20 percent) held 50 percent of AbilityOne projects and 80 percent of AbilityOne sales.

Program officials from all levels, as well as some of the affiliates themselves, told us that small and mid-size affiliates may struggle to compete for AbilityOne projects for a variety of reasons. For example, they told us that small affiliates cannot devote as many resources to business development or may only have the capacity to compete for projects in their local area. Affiliates also said that CNAs may not select them because of a perceived lack of work experience in a new line of business. Indeed, one affiliate told us it provides janitorial services and, despite efforts to expand into other businesses, it could not persuade its CNA to consider it for anything other than janitorial contracts. AbilityOne and CNA officials told us that while they try to give opportunities to smaller, less experienced firms, opportunities for smaller affiliates may be reduced when other factors are taken into account, such as a federal customer's preference for a larger, more experienced contractor.

The AbilityOne Commission Has Final Approval of Project Prices, but Procedures Could Be Strengthened

The Commission's Review and Approval of Price Recommendations for New Projects Lacks Transparency

While the AbilityOne Commission is ultimately responsible for determining the fair market price of projects in the program, it permits the CNAs, affiliates, and federal customers to negotiate pricing and recommend a fair market price for each project.[38] Commission guidance defines a fair market price as the price agreed upon by a buyer and seller, with neither under any compulsion to buy or sell and both having reasonable knowledge of relevant facts.[39] In addition, the Commission recognizes that providing jobs to people who are blind or have severe disabilities may necessitate employing a less than fully productive workforce, which could raise an affiliate's costs. As a result, according to Commission staff, a project's price under the AbilityOne Program is not necessarily the lowest possible price, but it also isn't the highest possible price. Commission guidance holds that the fair market price should include the CNA fee.

The process for determining the price of a project begins when an affiliate and federal customer are developing a potential project for the program and ends when that project is added to the Procurement List (see fig. 6).

---

[38]See 41 U.S.C. § 8503(b) and 41 C.F.R. § 51-2.7(a).

[39] AbilityOne Commission, *Procurement Guide* (Arlington, VA.: May 21, 2012), p. 18.

Figure 6: AbilityOne Commission's Pricing Review Process for Projects Proposed as Additions to the Procurement List

Step 1

Negotiate price during development of potential project

| CNAs | Affiliates | Federal customers |

- Affiliates and federal customers conduct market research to document a fair market price
- CNAs can offer technical assistance
- All three exchange information and attempt to arrive at a fair market price that both the affiliate and federal customer accept.

Negotiations should cover:
- Initial price for the base period of the project
- Mechanism to revise the price for follow-on periods (if applicable)

Yes ← **Has agreement on price been reached?** → No

Step 2

CNA assembles and reviews a package (including the negotiated pricing) which it submits to the Commission recommending that a project be added to the procurement list

CNA recommendation package includes:
- The initial price and the price review mechanism
- Supporting documentation from CNA, affiliate, and federal customer

Stop developing potential project

Step 3

Commission staff review the entire recommendation package, including price, and ask CNAs, affiliates, or federal customers for additional information if necessary

Commission staff review the package

If Commission staff do not agree with the price:
- project development can stop
  or
- negotiations re-open

Disapproved

If Commission staff agree with the price and endorse the project.
- Post Notice of intent to Federal Register
- 30 days for public to comment on proposal
- Recommend project approval

Approved →

Step 4

Commission members review and vote
- ✔ Vote on suitability of project for AbilityOne Program
- ✔ Vote to accept or reject the price

Disapproved

Approved →

Step 5

Project is added to the AbilityOne program

Federal customer submits order, affiliate provides it, and the federal customer pays for it

Source: GAO analysis of AbilityOne data.

Commission staff review the CNA pricing package in step 3 of the process. This review is a key control intended to ensure a fair market price. Between January 1, 2012 and December 10, 2012, the Commission received 336 new packages for price review. As shown in figure 7, staff recommended 78 to Commission members for final approval (23 percent). Staff rejected the pricing proposed in the other 258 pricing packages (77 percent), primarily because of insufficient documentation, but in some instances because they found the price too high. The CNAs and affiliates have the option of revising and resubmitting the rejected packages. After working with the CNAs, affiliates, and customers, as necessary, to produce better documentation or a revised price, staff recommended that Commission members approve the revised packages of 116 proposals. For the last several years, the Commission has approved all pricing packages the staff have recommended because they agreed with their staffs' recommendations.

Figure 7: Staff Decisions on the 336 New Pricing Packages, Jan. 1, 2012 – Dec. 10, 2012

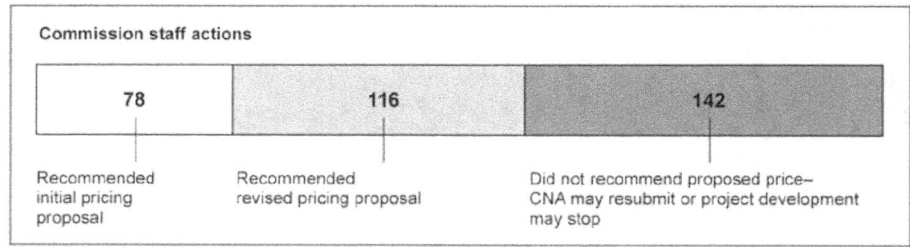

Source: GAO analysis of AbilityOne data.

Commission staff told us that they consider various factors when reviewing recommended prices, such as whether negotiations between the federal customer and affiliate are sufficiently documented. Staff also told us that they conduct research to determine whether the recommended price in a project addition package conforms with the pricing for similar goods and services available from public sources, and if not, whether the project addition package contains a sufficient explanation for these differences. Commission staff also told us that they conduct these reviews in accordance with written policies and procedures, but acknowledged that these instructions are not sufficiently explicit and transparent. Such limitations can make it difficult for the CNAs and affiliates to understand how and why decisions are made. CNA managers and some affiliates told us, for example, that they sometimes do not understand the Commission's price reviewing procedures and by extension, its reasons for rejecting prices. This lack of understanding about Commission reviews of recommended prices may partially explain the relatively high rejection rate of initial packages (see fig. 7). More explicit and transparent written policies and procedures on pricing reviews might include, for example, a checklist of what Commission staff should look for when assessing prices and a list of red flags that could indicate when recommended prices might be too high. Clearly-communicated price review procedures, including a discussion about the protocols the Commission uses to review pricing packages, could result in better-prepared pricing packages and therefore fewer rejections and less rework.

The Commission's Pricing Revision Process Has Not Ensured Approval of All Price Revisions

According to AbilityOne policy, all projects that extend beyond a single contract period must include a mechanism for adjusting the price. All parties involved—the affiliate, the federal customer, the CNAs, and the Commission—must agree on the mechanism. According to CNA officials, periodic negotiations between the affiliate and the customer are the most common price revision mechanism.[40] If a price revision conforms to the originally approved mechanism, the affiliate and customer implement the revision without seeking Commission approval or submitting documentation of the revision to the Commission. However, if the change in price does not conform to the originally approved mechanism, Commission policy directs affiliates to prepare a price revision request package, which the CNA submits to the Commission for staff approval.[41]

Between January 1, 2012, and December 10, 2012, Commission staff reviewed 569 packages for non-conforming price revisions (see fig. 8). Commission staff initially approved 216 of these packages (38 percent) and, after a subsequent review, approved an additional 157. Commission staff rejected 196 of the price revision packages, none of which had been

---

[40] Allowable price change mechanisms for products include (1) conducting a new round of market research and negotiating a new price; (2) a price index related to the major raw material or the end product; (3) an adjustment based on price changes published quarterly; and (4) market surveys comparing AbilityOne retail prices to commercial retail prices for similar commercial products.

[41] Common reasons for nonconforming price revisions are a change in the scope of work of a project, such as adding new equipment or a new facility to be served, or unanticipated, rapid changes in the price of raw materials.

GAO-13-457 Review of the AbilityOne Program

resubmitted at the time of our review. Commission staff told us that they might reject a price revision for a variety of reasons. Staff might see an anomaly in the request, such as a price that is increasing much faster than either (1) the original terms of the contract specified for future year price changes or (2) research indicates that it should be changing. Affiliates and their federal customers have the option to resubmit their requests with additional information or clarifications.

Figure 8: Staff Decisions on the 569 Price Revision Packages, Jan. 1, 2012 – Dec. 10, 2012

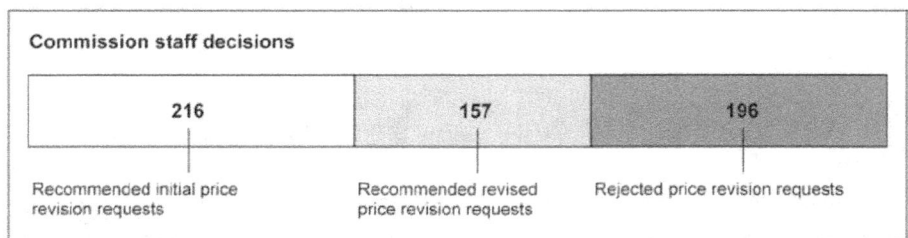

Source: GAO analysis of AbilityOne data.

Commission staff and CNA officials reported that they do not have procedures in place to ensure that affiliates comply with the policy that affiliates report to the Commission, through their CNA, any price revisions that do not conform with approved contract pricing mechanisms. If the Commission becomes aware of unreported price revisions, staff told us that they contact the affiliate and federal customer to attempt to resolve the situation, typically by asking for an immediate price revision package. Commission staff told us that unreported price revisions are a recurring problem, and provided us with three examples of price increases that should have been reported between 2 months and 19 years ago. Although they were not able to estimate the number of times such unreported increases occurred, they said that its recurring nature causes them concern. CNAs collect information on current prices, but the Commission does not require them to submit this information to the Commission. If the Commission had this information, it could electronically compare the current prices to the data it maintains on the approved prices and thus have assurances that controls were met. Failure to submit price revision requests to the Commission before raising prices (1) negates the Commission's internal controls that ensure that affiliates are charging fair market prices and (2) means that the Commission does not have accurate data regarding the prices that are actually being used within the program.

Conclusions

The AbilityOne Program is one of many federal programs designed to help people with disabilities find employment. It is the single largest source of employment for the blind and others with severe disabilities. This program's unique public-private structure was set up more than seven decades ago when federal purchasing was simpler and much smaller in scale. Today, billions of federal procurement dollars flow through the program every year and tens of thousands of people who are blind or have severe disabilities are employed through it.

The Commission's oversight of the CNAs is hampered by limitations in its monitoring procedures and in its authority over their operations. Developing a written agreement between the Commission and each CNA that specifies key expectations for the CNAs and oversight mechanisms could improve program accountability. It would be important to work to achieve an agreement within a reasonable period of time, such as 18 months. In the event that an agreement cannot be reached, it is important to identify in advance appropriate next steps for program changes by the Commission to establish adequate oversight and accountability for the AbilityOne program.

In addition, there are specific areas where the Commission needs to establish adequate oversight procedures to better help ensure program integrity, transparency, and effectiveness. These include:

- obtaining reports from CNAs on alleged misconduct and internal control violations to ensure that any appropriate corrective actions are taken,
- overseeing CNA procedures for assigning projects to affiliates to help ensure transparency and equity,
- developing more explicit and transparent written protocols for pricing reviews, and
- reviewing pricing packages to ensure fair market value.

Finally, the AbilityOne program does not have an independent IG. Without an independent IG, this major procurement program lacks an office to independently audit and investigate waste, fraud, and abuse and to make recommendations for enhancing program integrity and operations.

Matter for Congressional Consideration

To enhance program effectiveness, efficiency, and integrity in the AbilityOne Program, Congress may wish to consider establishing an independent inspector general for the program with the authority to audit and investigate the Commission and the CNAs.

Recommendations for Executive Action

To promote greater accountability for program effectiveness, efficiency, and integrity, the Chairperson of the U.S. AbilityOne Commission should direct the AbilityOne Commission to enter into a written agreement with each CNA within reasonable established time frames, such as within 18 months. The agreements should establish key expectations for each CNA and mechanisms for the Commission to oversee their implementation and could cover, among other things:

- expenditures of funds,
- performance goals and targets,
- governance standards and other internal controls to prevent fraud, waste, and abuse,
- access to data and records,
- consequences for not meeting expectations, and
- provisions for updating the agreement.

If the Commission is unable to enter into such a written agreement with either CNA, the Commission should take steps to designate a CNA that is willing to enter into such an agreement or seek legislation that would require such an agreement as a prerequisite to designation as a CNA.

To further improve oversight and transparency in the AbilityOne Program, the Chairperson of the U.S. AbilityOne Commission should:

- Routinely obtain from the CNAs any audits and reports of alleged misconduct or other internal controls violations, and information on corrective actions taken by the CNAs.
- Take additional action to better ensure that the CNAs' processes of assigning projects to affiliated agencies result in a transparent and equitable distribution. Such action could include one or more of the following:

  - further developing its policy to specify procedures CNAs should follow to ensure equity and transparency in project assignment decisions,
  - developing protocols for how the Commission will review CNA project assignment procedures to ensure their alignment with the Commission's policy, or
  - performing a study to determine if and how the distribution of projects among affiliates affects the number of jobs for people who are blind or have severe disabilities.

- Develop more explicit and transparent written procedures for how Commission staff review pricing packages and clearly communicate these procedures to affiliates and the CNAs. Such communication

might also highlight the most common reasons that pricing packages are rejected by Commission staff.
- Require the CNAs to provide current pricing information to enable the Commission to better identify instances when current prices differ from approved prices.

Agency and CNA Comments and Our Evaluation

We provided a draft of this report to the AbilityOne Commission, NIB, and NISH for review and comment. The Commission's comments are reproduced in appendix II, NIB's comments are reproduced in appendix III, and NISH's comments are reproduced in appendix IV. Technical comments from all three agencies were incorporated as appropriate.

In their written comments, the Commission and the two CNAs agreed with our matter for Congressional consideration and recommendations for executive action. They also provided additional information and disagreed with several findings. We subsequently modified the report in a few places to provide further clarification.

With regard to our matter for Congressional consideration about establishing an independent Inspector General (IG) for the program, the Commission concurred that there are benefits to having an independent entity conduct audits where needed. The Commission added that in its view, the creation of an IG would have to be budget neutral given the already scarce program funding for the Commission.

The Commission concurred with our recommendation to enter into a written agreement with each CNA and added that it will pursue these agreements once it has updated and enhanced its regulations to describe its authority and oversight with respect to the CNAs. The Commission added that it anticipates completing the written agreements in 18 to 24 months.

The Commission concurred with our recommendation to routinely obtain from the CNAs any audits and reports of alleged misconduct or other internal control violations, and information on corrective actions taken by the CNAs. The Commission added that it will establish or enhance and disseminate policies and procedures regarding CNA oversight and internal controls and anticipates that this will be completed in fiscal year 2014.

While NIB agreed with our recommendations to the Commission, NIB disagreed with our finding that the Commission has limited control over CNA spending. NIB highlighted several tools which it believes show that the Commission's controls are sufficient, such as the Commission's ability to set fee limits for the CNAs and provide guidance for, and review of, CNA budgets and performance. The report discusses these tools and presents evidence as to why we believe they are not sufficient for the Commission to oversee CNA spending. Both CNAs cited other controls that contribute to the oversight of their budgets. We cited examples of these other controls in the report, including IRS reporting requirements for nonprofit agencies and such CNA internal controls as undergoing annual independent financial audits. However, IRS and CNA internal controls cannot replace Commission oversight because the Commission is the entity that is most knowledgeable about the program's regulations and is ultimately responsible for ensuring compliance with these regulations and for the stewardship of the program.

The Commission and the two CNAs commented on CNA reserve levels. The Commission provided some additional clarification on its written guidance for reserves and actions taken, which we incorporated into the report. NISH disagreed with the statement that the CNAs have been accumulating reserve funds. However, our analysis of certified financial statements for NISH and NIB shows that (1) the annual reserves for NISH for fiscal years 2008 to 2012, as well as its reserve projection for fiscal year 2013, continued to grow and (2) NIB's reserves declined slightly in 2011and 2013 (see fig. 3). NISH also disagreed with the statement that the CNAs have not provided the Commission with financial analyses that support their levels of reserves and reserve policies. However, the statement in the report to which NISH refers actually focuses on actions of the Commission and we have clarified this in the report. This statement indicates that the Commission has not developed guidance about what the CNAs should consider when setting reserve policies nor determined what financial information the CNAs should provide to it to fully support their reserve levels. NISH and NIB cited the criteria they took to establish their reserve policies and levels in their comments.

NISH disagreed with the Commission's position that the Commission lacks the authority to require and enforce program improvements. During the course of our work, Commission officials noted that the Commission has very little explicit authority to regulate the CNAs and, as a result of this lack of authority, said they have not taken additional action to expand the Commission's oversight in ways that may be beneficial to the program. They said that, without additional oversight tools, they have few ways to enforce regulations. For example, although they could remove a CNA as an administrator of the program for noncompliance or significantly reduce its fees, such approaches could be highly disruptive to the program and the people it serves. Thus, depending on the infraction in question, they could be reluctant to use them. Because an agency's interpretation of its regulatory authority under the laws it is charged with administering is generally to be afforded deference, we did not make any changes to our report. However, we note that it may be beneficial for the Commission to engage with NISH on this issue as it takes steps to implement our recommendations, particularly the one focusing on entering into written agreements.

NIB disagreed with our finding that the Commission has limited oversight and control over areas such as CNA performance, governance, and internal controls. NIB's comments on this topic generally provided additional information about NIB's governance structure and controls and did not directly address the Commission's level of authority and control. However, in response to NIB's comments, along with additional clarification from a NIB official, we revised the report to make clear that NIB does not allow board members who are executives or employees of a NIB affiliate to serve as a Board officer, but those individuals can serve on the Board.

The Commission agreed with our recommendation that it take additional action to ensure that CNAs' processes of assigning projects to affiliated agencies result in a transparent and equitable distribution. The Commission noted that it has already initiated a review of CNA assignment policies as part of a larger review of procedures across the entire AbilityOne Program and that it will build our recommendations into the deliberative process. The Commission added that the target completion date for this review and development of procedures is no later than June 2014.

Both CNAs disagreed that their processes for assigning projects to affiliates were not transparent. NIB stated that the primary factor it uses when making assignment decisions is the potential to positively impact employment for people who are blind and NISH stated that it ensures transparency through several actions, including posting all notices of project opportunities on its website. However, we continue to believe that greater transparency is needed for the reasons stated in the report, including to address the concerns of some affiliates that: (1) they do not understand how the CNAs prioritize the criteria used to evaluate their proposals; (2) NISH applies its criteria inconsistently across its regions, and (3) NIB does not notify all of its affiliates about potential project opportunities it is considering for the program. NISH also stated that it disagreed with what it believed to be our assessment that CNA assignment processes are biased. We did not, however, state that these processes are biased; rather, we stated that some affiliates view them as biased. Greater transparency can help organizations address concerns of bias. NISH also provided additional information about its assignment processes that we incorporated in the report as appropriate.

The Commission and NISH provided comments about the distribution of projects among affiliates. The Commission noted that it will increase its emphasis and attention to mentoring the smaller affiliates so that they can more fully participate in the program. The Commission also suggested that we note that factors other than an affiliate's size can influence the number of projects affiliates are assigned in the program. We agree, but did not make any revisions to the report in this regard because we had already discussed such factors in the draft. NISH noted that it assigned more projects to its smaller affiliates in fiscal year 2012 than in prior years. However, because it is not clear how the distribution of projects among affiliates affects the creation of employment opportunities for people who are blind or have severe disabilities, it is not currently known whether assigning more projects to smaller affiliates is the most effective path for the program to pursue.

The Commission suggested that we modify the wording of our finding on the extent of the Commission's knowledge about how project assignment affects employment opportunities for its target population. The Commission noted that, while it is presented with information on the number of employment opportunities a proposed project will generate, it does not track the number of overall employment opportunities realized. In response, we revised the wording to clarify that the Commission does not track how the program's distribution of projects affects job creation for its target population. NIB reiterated several aspects about the process of adding projects to the Procurement List. In response to these comments we now more explicitly note that the Commission relies on CNA recommendations when adding projects to the Procurement List and votes on whether to approve CNA-recommended affiliates as project providers at the Procurement List addition stage.

The Commission agreed with our two recommendations for Commission actions to improve pricing reviews. However, the Commission took exception with our statement that Commission staff do not have written policies and procedures for reviewing pricing packages. The Commission stated that staff do have such written instructions and we confirmed this statement and revised the report to incorporate this information. Nonetheless, the Commission agreed with our assessment that its pricing review procedures are not sufficiently explicit or transparent and that this can make it difficult for the CNAs and affiliates to prepare acceptable pricing packages. The Commission noted, however, that the extent to which Commission reviews of pricing packages can be transparent is limited by the fact that such reviews are often based upon sensitive information that is not releasable to the CNAs or affiliates. We agree, but continue to believe that the Commission can increase the transparency of its pricing review processes.

As agreed with your offices, we will send copies to the appropriate congressional committees, the Chairperson of the U.S. AbilityOne Commission, the President and CEO of NISH, the President and CEO of NIB, and other interested parties. In addition, this report will be available at no charge on the GAO web-site at http://www.gao.gov.

If you or your staff members have any questions regarding this report, please contact me at (202) 512-7215 or sherrilla@gao.gov. Contact points for our Offices of Congressional Relations and Public Affairs may be found on the last page of this report. GAO staff who made major contributions to this report are listed in appendix V.

Andrew Sherrill

Andrew Sherrill
Director,
Education, Workforce and Income Security Issues

Appendix I: CNA Operating Expenses for Fiscal Year 2012 (in millions)

Table 1: NISH Operating Expenses for Fiscal Year 2012 (in millions)[a]

Type of Expense	NISH costs
Grants[b]	$2.90
Personnel	
Compensation of current officers, directors, trustees, and key employees	2.42
Other salaries and wages	32.45
Pension plan accruals and contributions	2.95
Other employee benefits[c]	7.09
Payroll taxes	2.43
Subtotal for Personnel	**47.34**
Fees for non-employee services	
Management	0.00
Legal	0.98
Accounting	0.18
Lobbying	0.32
Professional fund raising	0.00
Investment management fees	0.16
Other	5.20
Subtotal for non-employee fees	**6.84**
Advertising and promotion	2.07
Offices expenses	2.11
Information technology	4.31
Occupancy	1.98
Travel	4.47
Conferences, conventions and meetings	1.85
Interest	0.02
Depreciation, depletion, and amortization	1.63
Insurance	0.18
Other expenses	
Bad debt	1.10
Miscellaneous	1.11
Total	**$77.92**

Source: GAO analysis of RS Form 990 data reported by the CNAs and additional information provided by NISH officials.

[a] The CNA fiscal year begins on October 1and ends on September 30.

[b] CNAs provide grants to their affiliates.

[c] Employee benefits include health, dental, life, and disability insurance.

[d] In response to NISH's clarification of its operational costs, we removed $31.57 million for subcontracting costs that are associated with federal contracts in which NISH was the prime

contractor. According to NISH officials, these costs are not required to be reported on the IRS Form 990 as operational costs and NIB did not do so.

Table 2: NIB Operating Expenses for Fiscal Year 2012 (in millions)[a]

Type of Expense	NIB costs
Grants[b]	$0.43
Personnel	
Compensation of current officers, directors, trustees, and key employees	1.41
Other salaries and wages	13.24
Pension plan accruals and contributions	1.11
Other employee benefits[c]	1.38
Payroll taxes	$1.04
Subtotal for Personnel	**18.18**
Fees for non-employee services	
Management	0.00
Legal	0.25
Accounting	0.10
Lobbying	0.00
Professional fund raising	0.00
Investment management fees	0.01
Other	2.18
Subtotal for non-employee fees	**2.54**
Advertising and promotion	2.73
Offices expenses	0.90
Information technology	0.91
Occupancy	1.23
Travel	1.12
Conferences, conventions and meetings	0.58
Interest	00.0
Depreciation, depletion, and amortization	1.08
Insurance	0.11
Other expenses (listed by NIB)	
Training	0.50
Service Bureau[d]	0.49
Dues and Subscriptions	0.49
Inventory obsolescence	0.26
Other	0.60
Total	**$32.15**

Source: GAO analysis of RS Form 990 data reported by NISH and additional information provided by NIB officials.

[a] The CNA fiscal year begins on October 1 and ends on September 30.

[b] CNAs provide grants to their affiliates.

[c] Employee benefits include health, dental, life, and disability insurance.

[d] NIB's service bureau costs are for its outsourced data entry and call center.

Appendix II: Comments from the U.S. AbilityOne Commission

U.S. ABILITYONE COMMISSION

May 10, 2013

703-603-7740
FAX 703-603-0655

1401 S. Clark Street, Suite 10800
Arlington, Virginia 22202-4149

Andrew Sherrill, Director
Education, Workforce, and Income Security
U.S. Government Accountability Office
441 G Street, N.W., Room 5942
Washington, D.C. 20548

Re: Agency Comments on Draft Report GAO-13-457

Dear Mr. Sherrill:

Thank you for the opportunity to provide comments on the subject report. The report favorably reflects the efforts of your staff to learn and understand the unique public-private structure of our program, as well as our business practices. However, we do believe there are several areas that need further clarification. They are detailed below:

(a) The report states under *Establishing a Policy on Appropriate Reserve Levels* on page 10: "Moreover, the Commission has not provided written guidance to the CNAs about what they should consider when setting their reserve policies…"

The Commission requires that CNA business plans include a report on levels of reserves and provide an explanation of how they will use any surplus revenue to accomplish strategic goals identified by the Commission, including employment growth. As a result of reviewing these plans, concerns have been discussed, and levels of CNA reserves have been addressed in the past, such as through a reduction in the Commission-established CNA Fee Ceiling in FY 2007. The Commission's Business Excellence Subcommittee, which reviews CNA revenues and other metrics quarterly, has received verbal and written information on CNA reserve level policies. We note that in the past few years, the CNAs have increasingly invested their reserves balances in the development of new employment opportunities. The Commission concurs with the recommendation to document guidance on reserve policies in more specific, consistent terms and to establish procedures to more thoroughly review the outcomes no later than December 2013.

(b) The report states under *Enhancing Federal Oversight and Control…* on page 15: "One option to address this situation would be for the Commission to enter into a written agreement with each CNA that specifies key expectations for the CNA and mechanisms for the Commission to oversee their implementation."

Agency Comments on Draft Report GAO-13-457
Page 2

We concur with recommendation that a written agreement would be a useful tool in documenting performance and evaluation expectations. The Commission has long relied upon its regulations to specify the role of the CNAs. However, once the Commission updates and enhances its regulations to describe its authority and oversight relative to the CNAs, we will pursue written agreements.

(c) The report states under *Enhancing Federal Oversight and Control...* on page 16: "Another option to improve federal oversight of the program... would be to create an independent inspector general (IG) with the authority to audit and investigate the Commission and the CNAs."

We concur there are benefits to having an independent entity conduct audits where needed. However, Commission resources are needed to engage in business excellence, problem solving and strengthening the AbilityOne Program from a policy and oversight perspective. The creation of an IG would have to be budget neutral given the already scarce program funding. The Commission will continue to use other federal agency's IG services on a reimbursable basis.

(d) The report states under *The Commission Relies on the CNAs to Add Projects to the Program, But Has Not Resolved Concerns about How CNAs Assign Projects to Affiliates*, on page 16: "While a step in the right direction, this [the Commission's] policy may be ineffective in several ways."

The Commission had already initiated a more detailed review of the project assignment and other procedures used across the AbilityOne Program. We will build recommendations into our deliberative process as we continue the review and develop procedures. The target completion date for this review and development of procedures/policies is no later than June 2014.

(e) On page 23 the heading is: *The Commission Does Not Know How Project Assignment Affects Employment Opportunities for its Target Population.*

We believe a more accurate heading for this section would be, "*The Commission Does Not Track How Project Assignment Affects Employment Opportunities for its Target Population.*" We would also like to provide some context. Actions presented for Commission approval include the number of employment opportunities that action will generate; but, the Commission relies on CNA data to track the number of overall employment opportunities realized. We use Census data to assess unemployment levels for our target population, compared to program employment, regarding the effect of project assignments. We agree with the recommendation and intend to track this information more closely by the end of FY 2013.

On page 24 and illustrated in Figure 5: *Distribution of Projects among Different-Sized Affiliates*, the report speaks to the distribution of projects among differed sized affiliates. However, the report should note that the number of AbilityOne projects performed by a nonprofit agency and the selection of a designated nonprofit agency are based on several variables, not all of which are tied to the size of the nonprofit agency.

Agency Comments on Draft Report GAO-13-457
Page 3

Other considerations include nonprofit agency's location (particularly for service assignments), the number of years the nonprofit agency has participated in the AbilityOne Program, and the nonprofit agency's business model (manufacturing, providing services, or a combination), among other factors. The CNAs have performed analyses on distribution which the Commission routinely obtains and reviews. We agree that distribution of work across nonprofit agencies has benefits and will increase our emphasis and attention to mentoring the smaller nonprofit agencies and fostering their ability to participate in AbilityOne opportunities.

(f) The report states, "The *Commission Has Final Approval of Project Prices, but Procedures Could be Strengthened*".

We concur that the Commission procedures can be strengthened and have initiated actions to do so. In this area, several key actions we have taken should be noted: we have reviewed Commission memoranda (previously used as policy); deleted, updated, and revised pricing policy; and are now focusing on strengthening and communicating standard operating procedures.

(g) With regard to pricing under the section beginning on page 25: *The Commission's Review and Approval of Price Recommendations for New Projects Lacks Transparency*, page 27 reads: "Commission staff, however, do not have written policies and procedures detailing how they review pricing packages; and this lack of documentation reduces transparency..."

We believe a more accurate statement would be, "Commission staff should make its written policies and procedures detailing how they review pricing packages more explicit and transparent." We agree that explicit and transparent policies and procedures are important.

With respect to written procedures, the Commission uses written pricing instructions for reviewing AbilityOne products and services. The staff prepares an Excel spreadsheet for each pricing action that clearly outlines and documents the analysis undertaken to arrive at the pricing determination. The Commission's pricing memoranda detail the documentation required from Contracting Activities, CNAs and nonprofit agencies for pricing actions. As to transparency, these policies are available on our website, and we provide training and information on our policy in educational forums for contracting activities and nonprofit agencies. We also encourage parties to contact us with any questions or concerns as they prepare their pricing.

While the Commission supports maximum transparency in this area, there are some appropriate limits; namely, the Commission's price analysis and decisions are often based upon procurement sensitive information that is not releasable to the CNAs or nonprofit agencies.

(h) With regard to pricing under the section beginning on page 28 titled: *"The Commission's Pricing Revision Process Has Not Ensured Approval of All Price Revisions,"* the top of page 29 reads: "Commission staff and CNA officials reported that they do not have procedures in place to ensure that affiliates comply with requirements that affiliates report to the Commission ... any price revisions that do not conform to approved contract pricing mechanisms.

Agency Comments on Draft Report GAO-13-457
Page 4

We concur with the recommendation and will work with the CNAs, employing our strengthened policies and procedures, to promote timely and consistent submission of price revisions for Commission review. We anticipate having a solution in place by July 2014.

GAO Recommendation: Chairperson of the Commission should direct the AbilityOne Commission to enter into a written agreement with each CNA within reasonable established time frames such as 18 months.

Commission Response: We concur and will establish a written agreement based on publication of regulations, policy and procedure. At a minimum, our action will encompass the six areas noted by GAO in this report. We anticipate completion of a written agreement in 18-24 months. This schedule is based on concurrent implementation of recommendations herein and the requirements of the informal rulemaking process, which affords notice and comment periods.

GAO Recommendation: To further improve oversight and transparency in the AbilityOne Program, the Chairperson of the Commission should routinely obtain CNA audits, reports of alleged misconduct or other internal controls violations, and information on corrective actions taken ... [and] require CNAs to provide current pricing information to enable the Commission to better identify instances where current prices differ from approved prices.

Commission Response: We concur with the recommendation, and will establish or enhance and disseminate policies and procedures regarding CNA oversight and internal controls, assignment and allocation processes, pricing reviews and identification of nonconforming prices. We anticipate completion of these policies and procedures in FY 2014.

Lastly, it should be noted that the review team was professional, transparent and collegial in their performance of this review. As a result, the report provides a reasonable representation of improvements that we agree will strengthen the effectiveness and stewardship of the program. Again, thank you for the opportunity to review your draft and to provide comments. We look forward to receiving the final report.

Sincerely,

J. Anthony Poleo
Chairperson

NATIONAL INDUSTRIES FOR THE BLIND

1310 Braddock Place
Alexandria, VA 22314-1691
703-310-0500
www.nib.org

May 9, 2013

Mr. Andrew Sherrill
Director
Education, Workforce, and Income Security Issues
Government Accountability Office
441 G Street, NW
Washington, DC 20548

RE: "Employing People with Disabilities: Enhanced Oversight of the AbilityOne Program Needed" (GAO 13-457)

Dear Mr. Sherrill:

On behalf of the Board of Directors and staff of National Industries for the Blind (NIB), along with our 91 associated nonprofit agencies and the thousands of employees who are blind, we thank you and your team for your superior effort over the past 15 months to learn about the AbilityOne Program. By spending time with the employees who are blind and who benefit from the opportunities created by this program, you were able to experience firsthand the vital nature of the work we do.

We appreciate the opportunity to provide a response to your draft Report titled, "Employing People with Disabilities: Enhanced Oversight of the AbilityOne Program Needed."

Oversight

Your Report addresses the oversight of the U.S. AbilityOne Commission (Commission) over the Central Nonprofit Agencies (CNAs) in certain key areas. We respond to your comments on each area below:

1. GAO asserts that the Commission has "limited control over CNA spending."

As the Report illustrates, the AbilityOne Program was created with "a unique public-private structure" in 1938. It remains today one of the best examples of how leveraging the distinct capabilities of diverse partners can accomplish important social goals with a minimal impact on the federal budget, and contribute a very strong net positive impact to the American taxpayer.

Mr. Andrew Sherrill
May 9, 2013

NIB is an independent 501(c)(3) nonprofit organization. As a charitable organization, NIB is subject to the oversight and scrutiny of the Internal Revenue Service, and we are confident that our financial controls and processes are of the highest caliber. Under the guidance of the NIB Board of Directors, an outside independent auditing firm performs an annual audit of the NIB financial statements in accordance with Generally Accepted Auditing Standards (GAAS). NIB consistently operates with the best practices relative to internal controls, including our adherence to ISO quality standards as an ISO 9001-certified organization.

The Commission has the necessary authority and control over CNA spending as it sets the fee ceiling, which determines the maximum amount of fee that the CNAs may collect from the nonprofit agencies. Further, the Commission reviews the CNA budgets annually, and receives a quarterly report detailing key business metrics.

The Commission also directs the manner in which the CNAs provide their budget exhibits, reviews AbilityOne Program initiatives that the CNAs fund, and approves those non-inherently governmental functions that NIB performs in support of the Commission on behalf of the program. Additionally, the Commission establishes the fair market price for all products and services that are added to the Procurement List and is provided a business case that identifies anticipated sales for all these projects. NIB respectfully contends that this aggregation of financial levers and controls is sufficient for the Commission to ensure that programmatic goals are appropriately funded and that expenditures of funds are directed toward program objectives. NIB believes the Commission has the necessary authority and controls to ensure appropriate oversight of the CNAs.

The Report includes mention of NIB's financial reserves. The NIB Board maintains a very structured policy on reserves to ensure that NIB effectively balances environmental risks with our mission of enhancing economic and personal independence of persons who are blind, primarily through employment. As the Report notes, reserves are critical to ensure that sufficient funds are available to meet changing revenue requirements – such as those created by the uncertain conditions we are currently experiencing due to the volatility in the federal budget process.

Over the past five years, the NIB Board utilized reserves to invest in new programs designed to grow the AbilityOne Program and increase employment and career advancement for people who are blind. Examples include our Business Leaders Program, which prepares high-potential individuals who are blind for managerial opportunities. Further, these investments have allowed us to create high-skilled employment in the services arena by leveraging assistive technology for people who are blind.

2. GAO asserts that the Commission has "limited authority over CNA performance management, governance standards, and other internal controls."

A robust oversight and advocacy program has consistently been a primary objective of NIB, as we believe it provides the transparency necessary for a strong public-private partnership to succeed. Our governance structure enables the NIB Board to stay in touch with the needs of our associated agencies, while also benefitting from the broader perspectives, skills and experiences found outside the NIB network.

The Report may give the impression that both CNA Boards may be chaired by an associated agency director. Since our creation in 1938, the NIB Board has been chaired by a director from the private sector. Moreover, to avoid any potential conflicts of interest, NIB Bylaws allow only private-sector directors to be elected as officers, and the Board consistently follows a well-documented and rigorous Conflict of Interest Policy.

National Industries for the Blind Response to GAO 13-457   Page 2 of 4

Mr. Andrew Sherrill
May 9, 2013

3. GAO asserts that the Commission "relies on the CNAs to add projects to the program, but has not resolved concerns about how CNAs assign projects to affiliates."

Responsibility for project assignment is a core duty that the Commission delegates to the CNAs. The primary factor that the NIB staff relies on when making assignments is the potential to positively impact employment of people who are blind. The Commission ultimately and independently determines which projects are suitable for addition to the Procurement List. It should be noted, that in the approval process, the Commission also independently approves the selection of the associated nonprofit agency selected to do the work.

4. GAO asserts that the Commission "has final approval of project prices, but procedures could be strengthened."

We agree that the program would benefit from written protocols for pricing reviews that are sufficient for establishing the fair market price. NIB would encourage and support policies that are reasonable, adhere to generally accepted policies and procedures for price determinations used by the federal government for commercial products and services, and are applied consistently across the program. In instances where the federal agency contracting officers negotiate the prices to an acceptable conclusion with appropriate documentation, we believe it is advisable that the Commission accept these prices as representing a "fair market" determination by the federal government. The contracting officers making these determinations are educated and trained in this specific process.

NIB supports the Commission's efforts to establish FAR-based processes to follow when contracting agencies agree to place a product or service on the Procurement List. This structured, formal process would ensure acquisition officials are provided appropriate guidance on the project addition process. In the same fashion that the SBA has provided policies and procedures to acquisition professionals regarding the 8(a) set-aside program, the Commission should do the same for AbilityOne.

Recommendations

Your Report concludes with several recommendations that we address individually below.

1. As a matter for Congressional consideration, GAO recommends the establishment of an independent Inspector General (IG) with authority to audit and investigate the U.S. AbilityOne Commission and the CNAs for waste, fraud and abuse.

NIB Response: NIB believes that the concept of an independent IG bears consideration. We believe this could help ensure all components of the program are operating with the highest degree of integrity and compliance with the JWOD statute and accompanying regulations. We further recommend the scope of the duties of an IG includes ensuring that all federal agency procurement practices adhere to the JWOD statute.

2. GAO recommends that the U.S. AbilityOne Commission establish adequate oversight procedures to ensure program integrity, transparency and effectiveness in certain key areas.

NIB Response: NIB supports this recommendation and believes that clearly-written policies and procedures offer greater transparency, integrity and consistency for the program. We believe the NIB policies and practices in this area are sound and could serve as models for the entire program.

National Industries for the Blind Response to GAO 13-457   Page 3 of 4

Mr. Andrew Sherrill
May 9, 2013

NIB agrees that transparency and oversight is paramount when assigning projects to associated agencies. We believe that current NIB policies and procedures are appropriate and thorough in this area, and our track record validates this statement.

We support the Commission's need to establish FAR-based procedures to follow when contracting agencies agree to place a product or service on the Procurement List. NIB believes the Commission has a fundamental responsibility to educate, inform, monitor and direct federal acquisition officials on the requirements of the program.

> 3. GAO recommends the development of a written agreement between the U.S. AbilityOne Commission and each CNA specifying key expectations.

NIB Response: NIB agrees that a written agreement between the Commission and each CNA that specifies key expectations for both the CNA and the Commission could improve program accountability.

NIB would also endorse a collaborative process to clarify and outline roles and responsibilities for the CNAs, the Commission and the associated NPAs. Further, we would support the establishment of performance goals for all program participants. To this end, and in an effort to accomplish the desired outcomes of greater accountability, NIB recommends that a working group be created, comprised of representatives from NIB, NISH and the U.S. AbilityOne Commission, to jointly develop an implementation plan for the recommendations above.

Conclusion

As we enter our 75th year of creating quality employment opportunities for people who are blind, we are grateful for the thoroughness and sensitivity with which you and your staff conducted your review. We appreciate that you recognize the importance of this program in serving a population with a staggering 70% unemployment rate and we look forward to working collaboratively with the U.S. AbilityOne Commission and the United States Congress to move this program forward for the benefit of the people we serve.

Sincerely,

Kevin A. Lynch
President and CEO

Gary J. Krump
Chairman of the Board

Appendix IV: Comments from NISH

NATIONAL OFFICE

May 10, 2013

Mr. Andrew Sherrill
Director
Education, Workforce and Income Security Issues
U.S. Government Accountability Office
Washington, DC 20548

Dear Mr. Sherrill:

Thank you for the opportunity to review and comment on the U.S. Government Accountability Office (GAO) draft report entitled Employing People with Disabilities: Enhanced Oversight of the AbilityOne Program Needed (GAO-13-457).

As you are aware, NISH is an AbilityOne® authorized enterprise designated by the U.S. AbilityOne Commission® in accordance with 41 U.S.C. Chapter 85. NISH does not represent the U.S. AbilityOne Commission, an independent federal agency. NISH supports a national network of nearly 540 nonprofit agencies that participate in the AbilityOne Program. NISH nonprofit agencies provide training and employment opportunities for more than 125,000 people with significant disabilities, including nearly 45,000 individuals with significant disabilities through the AbilityOne Program.

In challenging economic times, NISH's role in generating employment opportunities for people with significant disabilities takes on even greater importance and requires significant effort. Last year, in partnership with nonprofit agencies, NISH added over 5,600 new jobs through new business and contract expansions. Procurement List additions included 116 new projects and should lead to an additional 2,000 jobs in the future. The average hourly wage reached an all-time high of $11.94. As the single largest source of employment for people who are blind or have significant disabilities in the United States, the AbilityOne Program provides tremendous value to the American taxpayer.

NISH appreciates the importance of ensuring the integrity of the AbilityOne Program and has long been committed to operating pursuant to strict accountability standards. In addition to implementing the standards required under Sarbanes-Oxley for nonprofit organizations, NISH has voluntarily adopted numerous aspects of the law's best practices required only for the for-profit sector. For example, in 2004, NISH's Board of Directors established an Audit Committee comprised of independent members that routinely retains external auditors to review and recommend improvements to NISH's internal controls. In 2012, at the encouragement of the Audit Committee's leadership, NISH's Board of Directors adopted key tenets of the Institute of Internal Auditors' standards for accountability.

NISH has reviewed GAO's draft report and supports the recommendations which we believe will further clarify expectations, enhance controls and oversight already in place, and improve policies and procedures which will increase employment opportunities for people with significant disabilities. The attached comments address the full report and provide several clarifications on certain statements

8401 Old Courthouse Road, Vienna, VA 22182
PHONE: 571.226.4660 FAX: 703.849.8916 EMAIL: info@nish.org

| William S. Coleman | Paul J. Atkinson | Brenda L. Yarnell | Frederick Beaman, III | E. Robert Chamberlin |
| Chair | Chair-Elect | Treasurer | Secretary | President and CEO |

Mr. Andrew Sherrill

which may be misunderstood as currently written. We appreciate the opportunity to share our views in furtherance of AbilityOne's critical mission.

NISH looks forward to working with the U.S. AbilityOne Commission to address the report recommendations and ultimately achieve our shared vision of employment for every individual with a significant disability.

NISH thanks the members of the GAO team for their professionalism in how they conducted this audit.

Sincerely,

E. Robert Chamberlin
President and CEO

Attachment

2

NISH COMMENTS (GAO-13-457)

ATTACHMENT

- **The Commission Has Limited Control Over CNA Spending (pg.6)**

We agree that the U.S. AbilityOne Commission™ (the Commission) has limited control over some aspects of CNA operations which is appropriate given that CNAs are independent 501(c)(3) entities. The Commission, however, has a level of input and resulting influence, not apparent in other socio-economic programs, over CNA corporate activities including: spending of funds, setting and managing programmatic growth goals and establishing policies and procedures to ensure proper controls.

As an example, NISH participates with the Commission in a multi-stage review as part of our annual business plan/budget approval process. This process begins with budget guidance from the Commission specifying areas of interest or focus, and a Business Excellence Subcommittee review of NISH's business plan. The review provides NISH an opportunity to clarify for the Commission how funds will be spent in implementation of the Program, to respond to questions and concerns, and to receive recommended changes. The Commission has the sole authority to designate central nonprofit agencies and set the fee ceiling. The fee-setting process serves as an incentive for NISH to specifically support or address areas highlighted in the budget guidance as well as respond to Commission concerns and recommendations. In fact, this report references statements made by Commission staff which indicate NISH continues to support Commission leadership in the direction and specific demands of the Program. It is also noteworthy that NISH has internal controls and audit practices fully compliant with Internal Revenue Service regulations, Sarbanes-Oxley provisions and Generally Accepted Accounting Principles.

- **Controlling Key CNA Cost Areas (pg. 8)**

We agree with the statement that the Commission has no immediate or direct control over the amount of CNA executive compensation. NISH and its network of nonprofit agencies, however, as Federal contractors are required to comply with the compensation guidelines set forth in Part 31 of the Federal Acquisition Regulation. NISH complies with Internal Revenue Service guidelines and, consistent with industry best practices, engages an independent compensation consultant to validate the reasonableness of executive compensation and confirm that no excess benefits occurred.

Additionally, NISH would like to offer further clarification around the Commission's proposed regulation on "Governance Standards for Central Nonprofit Agencies and Nonprofit Agencies Participating in the Javits-Wagner-O'Day Program" (November 12, 2004). The proposal was more expansive than just the executive compensation at the CNAs, rather it proposed to amend regulations impacting "nonprofit agencies awarded Government contracts under the authority of the JWOD Act, as well as central nonprofit agencies designated by the Committee and nonprofit agencies that would like to qualify for participation in the JWOD Program." The rule proposed comprehensive revisions to the AbilityOne Program including changing "the structure of the central nonprofit agency's or nonprofit agency's governing authority, such as its Board of Directors; auditing and reporting of the central nonprofit agency's or nonprofit agency's finances; executive compensation packages provided by the central nonprofit agency or nonprofit agency; and the central nonprofit agency's or nonprofit agency's conflict of interest policy."

It is important to note, per the proposed rule, these changes were prompted by "isolated instances of excessive compensation packages for nonprofit agency executives; a perceived lack of full disclosure in the financial reporting of nonprofit agencies and, the absence of formal guidelines to nonprofit agencies." The diverse business portfolio of the vast majority of nonprofit agencies includes work outside the AbilityOne Program and the federal contracting arena, such as broad-based rehabilitation programs and social enterprise activities. Many commented on the potential effect the proposed

1

NISH COMMENTS (GAO-13-457)

regulations would have on their ability to retain strong leadership capable of managing organizations which are often as complex as commercial entities. In a letter dated, August 24, 2005, the Commission communicated its decision to withdraw the proposed rule to allow time to better incorporate many of the public comments from 167 sources.

Establishing a Policy on Appropriate Reserve Levels (pg. 10)

NISH disagrees with the statement that the CNAs have been accumulating reserve funds and have not provided the Commission financial analyses that support levels of reserves and reserve policies. NISH budgets over the last several years have targeted a balanced or deficit budget. NISH has developed and implemented reserve policies to ensure financial sustainability and to provide the ability to make significant investments in the Program and grow employment for people with significant disabilities. The current reserve policy at NISH was established using benchmarked data and financial standards from other national not-for-profit organizations as provided by the biannual reports from ASAE®– The Center for Association Leadership. In prior years, financial reserves have directly contributed to NISH/AbilityOne jobs added to the Procurement List and NISH anticipates additional generation of jobs based on reserves allocated in Fiscal Year 2013. The reserve levels at NISH are reviewed at least annually by the NISH Board of Directors and reported to the Commission. As part of the fee deliberation process the Commission has statutory authority to adjust the CNA fee which impacts NISH's reserves.

Ensuring CNA Funding of Program Initiatives (pg. 11)

NISH disagrees with the concluding statement that the Commission lacks the authority to request and enforce Program improvements. Pursuant to 41 U.S.C. §8503(d)(1), the Commission "…may prescribe regulations regarding…other matters as necessary to carry out this chapter." NISH is unable to identify any initiative that we did not support in recent years.

Assignment of AbilityOne Program Projects (pg. 17)

NISH disagrees with statements that the process used by NISH to assign projects is not transparent and is biased. NISH has continually revised the distribution process over the last five years based on feedback from CRP and Federal customers. These improvements include posting opportunities in a system accessible by all CRPs. Postings include stated criteria applicable to the opportunity. Unsuccessful bidders are provided the opportunity to receive a debriefing addressing the strengths and weaknesses of their responses. In rare instances where a sole source award is based on Federal customer needs, a justification, in accordance with policy, is included in the above system to ensure transparency.

In the past several years NISH has continued to improve the project distribution process with regards to suitability, employment potential and customer satisfaction, actively incorporating customer feedback at every step of the process. The resulting improvements have resulted in 38 percent of total AbilityOne/NISH projects and 19 percent of total AbilityOne/NISH sales distributed to small NISH affiliates in Fiscal Year 2012 which demonstrates a clear improvement over the 24 percent of AbilityOne projects and 7 percent of AbilityOne sales as presented in this report.

2

Appendix V: GAO Contact and Staff Acknowledgements

GAO Contact	Andrew Sherrill (202) 512-7215 or sherrilla@gao.gov
Staff Acknowledgments	In addition to the contact named above, Assistant Director Bill Keller, Nancy Cosentino, Julie DeVault, Sara Pelton, and Paul Wright made significant contributions to this report. Assistance, expertise, and guidance were provided by Kurt Burgeson, David Chrisinger, Michele Grgich, Alex Galuten, Kristine Hassinger, Steve Lord, Mimi Nguyen, Jerry Sandau, William Shear, Walter Vance, Monique Williams, and William Woods.

GAO's Mission	The Government Accountability Office, the audit, evaluation, and investigative arm of Congress, exists to support Congress in meeting its constitutional responsibilities and to help improve the performance and accountability of the federal government for the American people. GAO examines the use of public funds; evaluates federal programs and policies; and provides analyses, recommendations, and other assistance to help Congress make informed oversight, policy, and funding decisions. GAO's commitment to good government is reflected in its core values of accountability, integrity, and reliability.
Obtaining Copies of GAO Reports and Testimony	The fastest and easiest way to obtain copies of GAO documents at no cost is through GAO's website (http://www.gao.gov). Each weekday afternoon, GAO posts on its website newly released reports, testimony, and correspondence. To have GAO e-mail you a list of newly posted products, go to http://www.gao.gov and select "E-mail Updates."
Order by Phone	The price of each GAO publication reflects GAO's actual cost of production and distribution and depends on the number of pages in the publication and whether the publication is printed in color or black and white. Pricing and ordering information is posted on GAO's website, http://www.gao.gov/ordering.htm. Place orders by calling (202) 512-6000, toll free (866) 801-7077, or TDD (202) 512-2537. Orders may be paid for using American Express, Discover Card, MasterCard, Visa, check, or money order. Call for additional information.
Connect with GAO	Connect with GAO on Facebook, Flickr, Twitter, and YouTube. Subscribe to our RSS Feeds or E-mail Updates. Listen to our Podcasts. Visit GAO on the web at www.gao.gov.
To Report Fraud, Waste, and Abuse in Federal Programs	Contact: Website: http://www.gao.gov/fraudnet/fraudnet.htm E-mail: fraudnet@gao.gov Automated answering system: (800) 424-5454 or (202) 512-7470
Congressional Relations	Katherine Siggerud, Managing Director, siggerudk@gao.gov, (202) 512-4400, U.S. Government Accountability Office, 441 G Street NW, Room 7125, Washington, DC 20548
Public Affairs	Chuck Young, Managing Director, youngc1@gao.gov, (202) 512-4800 U.S. Government Accountability Office, 441 G Street NW, Room 7149 Washington, DC 20548

www.ingramcontent.com/pod-product-compliance
Lightning Source LLC
Chambersburg PA
CBHW080543290526
45790CB00006B/2526